The Search for the Niger

by the same author

CAPTAIN MARRYAT AND THE OLD NAVY
THE NAVY AND THE SLAVE TRADE
CAPTAIN COOK
SIR FRANCIS DRAKE
WILLIAM DAMPIER
THE BRITISH SEAMAN
MR BARROW OF THE ADMIRALTY

The Search for the Niger

CHRISTOPHER LLOYD

Late Professor of History,
Royal Naval College, Greenwich

COLLINS

St James's Place · London · 1973

William Collins Sons & Co Ltd
London · Glasgow · Sydney · Auckland
Toronto · Johannesburg

First published 1973
© Christopher Lloyd 1973

ISBN 0 00 211742 8

Set in Monotype Baskerville
Made and Printed in Great Britain by
William Collins Sons & Co Ltd Glasgow

Contents

Introduction 9

1 The Mystery of the Niger 13

2 Mungo Park's First Expedition 27

3 The Death of Mungo Park 46

4 The Attack from the North 60

5 Hugh Clapperton 77

6 The Solution of the Mystery: The Landers 103

7 Upstream: Macgregor Laird 126

8 The Second Attempt: Allen and Trotter 146

9 The Travels of Dr Barth 161

10 Dr Baikie's Settlement 187

Chronology of Principal Events 209

Sources 210

Index 215

Illustrations

Africa by Abraham Ortelius, 1570   *facing page* 32
Mungo Park   32
Barbary and Nigritia by De L'Isle, 1700   33
René Caillié   33
D'Anville's map of 1749 (detail)   48
Sir Joseph Banks   48
Two Musicians   49
Crossing the Niger at Say   96
View of the Bahr Mandia oasis   96
Captain Hugh Clapperton   97
Richard Lander   112
A lancer of the Sultan of Begharmi   113

Lieutenant John Glover RN   *between pages* 152 and 153
The *Dayspring*
The confluence of the rivers Niger and Chadda
Dr Heinrich Barth
Dr Baikie
The *Quorra* aground near Lokoja

The author wishes to express his thanks to the London Library for much help over the illustrations.

Maps

The Travels of Mungo Park   33

Routes of Laing; Denham and Clapperton;
    Caillié   80

The Course of the Quorra and route, redrawn
    from Lander's narrative   112

The Expedition of Laird and Oldfield   133

The Travels of Henry Barth   168

Nigeria, showing places visited by Baikie   193

Introduction

The names of the explorers of East Africa – Burton and Speke, Baker and Grant, and above all Livingstone – are much better known than those who, in the preceding generation, penetrated West Africa in search of the Niger. The search for the sources of the Nile caught the imagination of the Victorian public, mainly because it combined advances in geographical knowledge with missionary activity. Their exploits were publicised in popular accounts and by the dramatic appearance of the explorers at meetings of the Royal Geographical Society, then at the height of its influence.

Apart from Mungo Park (best known on account of his Christian name), the earlier explorers of the Niger – Hugh Clapperton, the Lander brothers, Macgregor Laird, Henry Barth, Dr Baikie – lived at a time when African travellers were seldom celebrated in such a manner. The attention of those interested in exploration was at that time centred on efforts to discover a North West Passage round America. Though most of the explorers were deeply religious men, they were not missionaries, nor did the efforts to suppress the illegal Atlantic slave trade affect them directly. However much space was devoted to their efforts in heavy reviews like the *Edinburgh* or the *Quarterly*, it was nothing compared with the pictures of their successors in the *Illustrated London News*.

The search for the Niger from the 1790's to the 1860's was a concerted international effort, inspired by the African

Association, which was the predecessor of the Geographical Society, and carried out by British, French and German travellers. Begun through the enthusiasm of Sir Joseph Banks, the search was then organised by Sir John Barrow and its results were followed up by philanthropists like Fowell Buxton and merchants like Macgregor Laird. Hopes that a trade in palm oil would replace the traffic in slaves were intensified by the demands of an expanding economy in search of new markets to which the Niger promised to serve as a highway.

Throughout this period European travellers were handicapped by deficiencies in tropical medicine in an area where conditions are the most lethal in the world. Apart from the number of intrepid young men who perished at the hands of Muslim fanatics in the north, the search for the Niger is a sad but heroic record of deaths from fever, dysentery and other diseases, until Dr Baikie showed how the preventive use of quinine provided the key to the opening of the Dark Continent.

Our story is therefore that of individual travellers sent out, at first, by the African Association and later by the government. By their discoveries they established the course of the mysterious river until it was charted and some sort of settlement attempted in the interior of modern Nigeria as a consequence of advances in medical knowledge, that is to say after Baikie's long years of residence on the banks of the lower Niger in the middle of the nineteenth century. The story is told from the European point of view: what the Africans thought about it is not recorded. It is based on contemporary accounts, whether printed by the travellers themselves (and every Victorian traveller wrote a book), or still lying unpublished in the Public Record Office or the British Museum.

We begin with a sketch of the problem and an explanation why attempts to solve the mystery of the Niger were so long delayed. Mungo Park's great discovery of the upper waters of the river and his tragic fate are the first themes to be treated. We pass on to the problem of its course to the sea, as well as that of the fabled city of Timbuktu. Some explorers started their search from the north, thereby encountering the hitherto unknown empires of Sokoto and Bornu. Others, like René Caillié and Hugh Clapperton on his second expedition, came up from the south, until Richard Lander, the most modest and enterprising character in the story, solved the mystery of the lower Niger and its termination in the Bights of Benin and Biafra on his first two expeditions, though he was killed on the third.

Attempts to exploit his success and to trade on the river began with Macgregor Laird's first Niger expedition with the use of paddle steamers. The appalling casualties suffered on that tragic affair, as well as those of the second attempt to sail up the river from the delta, checked further progress for a decade, until Baikie's voyages up to the confluence of the Niger with the Benue, and his settlement there, bring the story to an end, because at the same time the travels of Heinrich Barth further north provided the first comprehensive account of the more civilised conditions prevailing in the heart of the unknown continent. The second stage of imperial expansion and the sordid political scramble for Africa towards the end of the century is no part of our story, which is one of individual courage and enterprise.

As an epitaph on these men one cannot do better than quote the words of Hakluyt's friend, John Pory, when in 1600 he translated the work of Leo Africanus, *A Geographical Historie of Africa, written in Arabicke and Italian by John Leo, a More:*

"As touching his exceeding great Travels, I marvell much how he ever should have escaped so manie thousands of imminent dangers. How often he was in hazard to have become captived, or to have his throte cut by the prauling

Arabians, and wilde Mores? And how hardly manie times escaped he the Lyons greedie mouth, and the devouring jawes of the Crocodile. . . ."

The reader's indulgence is asked for any inconsistency in the spelling of the names of smaller towns and villages: every traveller spelled them differently and many have disappeared from the map in the last hundred years.

1

The Mystery of the Niger

In the article on Africa in the second edition of the *Encyclopaedia Britannica*, which was published in 1778, the author
expresses his surprise that Europeans, "notwithstanding
their extraordinary and insatiable thirst after gold and
silver, should not have endeavoured to establish themselves
effectively in a country much nearer to them than either
America or the East Indies, and where the objects of their
desire are to be found in equal, if not greater plenty."
Unfortunately, in the map accompanying the article, the
Niger is not even shown.

Part of the reason for this neglect of West Africa was that
Europeans were too busy fighting among themselves over
the footholds which they established there in the first era of
European expansion – miserable spots from which the slave
trade was conducted, which changed hands regularly after
every war for two centuries. Moreover, the Africans jealously
preserved their independence, as well as the sources of supply
of slaves and gold. The absence of good harbours or navigable
rivers leading to the interior made communications impossible; nor in that deadly climate could white men follow
the tracks through forests impassable to wheeled vehicles and
even, because of the tsetse fly, to beasts of burden. It was
much easier to lie off the coast in a slaving vessel and wait
for Africans to bring their "black ivory" to them. Above all,
as the early Portuguese historian João de Barros lamented,
"It seems that for our sins, or for some inscrutable judgement
of God, in all the entrances of this great Ethiopia that we

13

sail along, He has placed a striking angel with a flaming sword of deadly fevers, who prevents us from penetrating into the interior to the springs of this garden, whence proceed rivers of gold that flow to the sea in so many parts of our conquest."

De Barros was referring to the coast of Guinea, the part of Africa best known to white men, because they took good care not to risk their lives by penetrating beyond the forts and trading stations strung along the coast. When the King of Portugal built the first of these white-washed castles at El Mina in 1481 he called himself Lord of Guinea, hoping to tap the alluvial gold found in Ashanti. Similarly, when the English African Company extended its operations from the Gambia to the Gold Coast they too hoped for gold and a coin first minted in 1662 was called a guinea.

It seems paradoxical that Africa was the first continent to be visited by white men in the process of European expansion overseas and yet was the last to be explored. Up to the end of the nineteenth century it remained the Dark Continent, the Unknown Continent, and its interior the Heart of Darkness. Early Portuguese navigators merely traced the coastal outline and their descendants, disappointed in the amount of gold they found, interested themselves solely in the coast of Guinea for slave trading purposes. England followed their example with the voyage of William Hawkins of Plymouth, the father of the better known Sir John, when in the middle of the sixteenth century he armed "a tall and goodly ship of his own" to transport negroes across the Atlantic. At first the English at the Gambia and the French at the Senegal were more interested in legitimate trade. In 1618 there was formed a Company for the Countries of Ginney and Binney in order to discover the secrets of the golden trade of the Moors. It found neither Moors nor gold, and the Gambia was explored rather than Guinea. On the second ship to be sent out by the Company (which was the predecessor of the Royal African Company) there was an intelligent young man called Richard Jobson, who has left us the earliest description of the Gambia, which became the starting point of the exploration of the Niger. When offered a "coffle" or string of slaves, he primly remarked that "We are a people who do not deal in such commodities, neither do we buy or sell one another, or any that have our own shape". Such an attitude was incomprehensible to Africans, nor was it long before the English, the French, the Dutch, the Danes and the Spanish took to shipping slaves as the Portuguese had long done. This was the Slave Coast proper, where in the eighteenth century British shipping predominated and the fortunes of Bristol and Liverpool were made.

The search for the Niger began in the Senegambia region because most people imagined that it flowed into the sea there. But neither the English on the Gambia nor the French on the Senegal travelled far up their respective rivers. When Francis Moore in 1738 published his *Travels into the Interior Parts of Africa* he was only describing a hundred miles of river which he thought was connected with the Niger. He did, however, give a kindlier picture of the Africans than was then current at home: "The behaviour of the Natives to strangers is not so disagreeable as people are apt to imagine; for when I went through any of their Towns, they almost all came to shake hands with me, except some of the Women, who having never seen a White Man, ran away from me as fast as they could." Mungo Park was to owe his life on many occasions to the friendliness of such negroes, whom the tawny Moors of the north regarded as belonging to an inferior race, though he would have agreed with Moore that many of their rulers practised "a cruelty and villainy which can scarcely be conceived."

Why did the Niger, which the natives called "the River of Rivers", remain the most mysterious of all the great rivers of the world up to little over a hundred years ago? Its unpredictable course over 2600 miles was partly to blame, rising as it does in West Africa close to the headwaters of the Gambia and the Senegal, flowing north-east towards the almost mythical Timbuktu, and then following a great bend southward until it is lost in the network of rivers forming its delta in the Bight of Benin. During its long course it flows through every type of landscape from the deserts of the north to the rain forests and mangrove swamps of southern Nigeria. Only parts of the river served as a means of communication, so that the inhabitants of the countries bordering its banks were as various in race, religion and language as the landscapes through which it passed. Peoples living only a few hundred miles apart were as ignorant of each other, and therefore of the river itself, as if they were separated by thousands of miles of ocean.

Hence misconceptions about the river were as various as its peoples and as baffling as the river is long. No one knew its true course, nor was there any agreement as to its name. Some said that it flowed west into the Senegal and thence into the Atlantic. Others were of the opinion that its course was easterly, until its waters evaporated somewhere in the unknown parts of Central Africa south of the Sahara. Herodotus thought it was a branch of the Nile. El Edrisi in the twelfth century called it the Nile of the Negroes. Leo Africanus four hundred years later described it as the upper part of the Senegal. At the beginning of the nineteenth century Mungo Park and Sir John Barrow thought it might form the upper part of the Congo. No one considered the possibility that it flowed into the Bight of Benin, or that the ill-famed swamps frequented by slave ships at the mouths of the Nun, the Brass, the Bonny might form its delta.

Part of the trouble in identifying a river of such length which flowed north, east and south, lay in the multiplicity of its names. Dr Baikie, the last of the explorers considered in this book, lists twenty-nine names for the main stream and nineteen for the Benue, its chief tributary. Ptolemy called it the Nigeir. Classical writers such as Pliny gave it the name of Niger because of its association with black people, though in fact the name is derived from the African word *n'ger-n-gereo* or *nigr*, meaning great river. Its upper reaches were known locally as the Joliba, its lower as the Quorra or Kwora, and there were twenty other rivers in the delta. Some called the Benue the Tchadda, from its supposed source in Lake Chad, others the Shary or Binue.

"Africa, as you know," Lord Chesterfield told his son early in the eighteenth century, "is divided into nine principal parts, which are Egypt, Barbary, Biledulgerid (Tunisia), Zaara (Sahara), Nigritia (western Sudan), Guinea (Gambia to Calabar), Nubia and Ethiopia. The Africans are the most ignorant and unpolished people in the world, little better than the lions and tigers and leopards and other wild beasts, which that country produces in great numbers." If he was using a standard map of the period, such as that by De L'Isle (which differed little from that by Mercator over a hundred years earlier), he would have seen the Niger rising in Lake Chad and flowing west through the state of Bornu to the kingdom of Timbuktu, where in the land of the Fulis (Fulani) it changed its name to Senegal and as such entered the ocean just north of the Gambia.

Mercator had thought more highly of the negroes than Lord Chesterfield, though neither of them ever saw one, apart from the black page boys who formed a fashionable adjunct to an eighteenth century household. According to him, their country was abundantly stored with gold and silver – which unknown country was not? "The aire is very healthful, so that if any man that had the French poxe did go thither, he would be surely cured." It seemed a long way to go in search of health, but at least this part of West Africa was better than the Land of Guinea, where "the aire is contrarie to the nature of our bodies, as well as by reason of the distemper, as for the raine which engendreth putrification and vermine."

There is, of course, a striking contrast between the savannah belt of the western Sudan, through which the upper Niger flows roughly from west to east, and the tropical rain forests of the south. It is a contrast not only of topography, vegetation and climate, but of race, religion and culture. The Moorish Muslim north, inhabited by Tuareg (the veiled people of the desert), and Fulani, looked north to the shores of Barbary and Morocco, which were reached by well-known trade routes across the Sahara to such places as Tripoli and Marakesh. A hundred years ago at least ten thousand negro slaves were still taken annually along these routes, half of them to Tripoli, the other half to Algiers or Morocco. The bones of many more lined the desert tracks, as European travellers testified when they began to try to reach the Niger from the north. In the pagan south, the land of the negroes whom the Moors despised, the slave trade went the other way, down through the forest to the coast and across the Atlantic.

It was in the northern area that most of the gold was to be found. Its secrets were jealously guarded, but from the dawn of history it was transported across the desert by "the golden trade of the Moors." Its source was the mythical Wangara, variously placed near Lake Chad or near Timbuktu a thousand miles west. The truth was, as Major Denham wrote when he discovered the former, that "all gold countries as well as people coming from a gold country are called Wangara." Here, along the banks of the upper Niger, arose legendary empires called Ghana and Mali, whose ruler is depicted on the Catalan map of 1375 as Lord of the Negroes of Guinea (meaning Ghana), holding a nugget of gold at Tenbuch (Timbuktu). No wonder he became confused with Prester John on the other side of the continent. When the search for the Niger began, the empire of Mali lay in ruins and the dominant power lay in the hands of the Fulani people, who abandoned their pastoral way of life to rule the whole area along the great bend of the river from Timbuktu to Katsina, as well as the rich Hausa states with their walled cities such as Kano and Sokoto. It was with the Fulani emirs that the early travellers had to contend. To the north-east of their empire lay the comparatively advanced Muslim state of Bornu, while to the south lay the negro Yoruba kingdoms, of which Benin is the most famous. For two centuries preceding the search for the Niger these states had declined or stagnated, until the Fulani invasions in the north and the abolition of the slave trade in the south brought to an end an era which has been called "the centuries of historical night."

The generation to which Mungo Park belonged obviously no longer believed the Gothic fables that this part of Africa was inhabited by Strapfoots, who crawled rather than walked, or mythical beasts such as the Pegasus, the Yale or the Mantichora, with its lion's body and scorpion's tail, its voice like a trumpet and its peculiar appetite for human flesh. None the less, their knowledge of the geography of the western Sudan was still based on the writings of El Edrisi in the twelfth century and Leo Africanus in the sixteenth.

Abu Abdullah Mohammed El Edrisi was the grandson of the Emir of Malaga and the leading geographer of his day. He found his way to the cosmopolitan court of King Roger of Sicily, so that his description of Africa is still known as the Book of Roger. It was not translated until 1619, when it appeared under the title of *Geographia Nubiensis*. According to him, the Nile of the Negroes rose from the same source as the Nile of Egypt, but flowed westwards across Central Africa into the Atlantic Ocean. It passed through the large and wealthy kingdom of Ghana, where Wangara was famed for its gold. England (it may be added in parenthesis), which was equally remote from his Sicilian background, is described as "set in the Ocean of Darkness. This country is most fertile;

its inhabitants are brave, active and enterprising, but all is in the grip of perpetual winter."

Leo Africanus was also born in Spain, being one of the last of the Moors before their expulsion. He was the son of wealthy parents living at Granada. At an early age he was sent to Africa, where he travelled widely until he was captured by Christian corsairs, who took him to Rome. Here Leo X patronised him and gave him the name by which he is now known. His *History and Description of Africa and the Notable Things therein contained* was translated into English by John Pory, a friend of Hakluyt, in 1600. There are two important misconceptions in the book which were to distort the European view of Africa for a long time to come. One was that Timbuktu was a fine city, the centre of Muslim culture and trade, inhabited by "people of a gentle and cheerful disposition, who spend a great part of the night singing and dancing through the streets," whose ruler dined off gold plate. It is easy to understand the glamour surrounding this secret city, but when René Caillié first saw it he found the place "nothing but a mass of ill-looking houses, built of mud."

A more serious error was his support of El Edrisi's opinion that "the river Niger passes through the middle of the country of the Blacks. The river rises in a desert called Seu, where it emerges from a great lake (Chad) and flows westward towards the ocean. Our geographers assert that the Niger is a branch of the Nile, which disappears underground and emerges from this lake. This is not true; we ourselves have navigated the river from Timbuktu in the east and followed the current to the kingdoms of Guinea and Mali, both of which lie to the west of Timbuktu." If, indeed, El Edrisi or Leo ever embarked on the river, this is an incomprehensible statement; nevertheless, the error was enshrined in all sixteenth and seventeenth century maps.

It remained for Mungo Park to discredit this westerly flow

of the river, but in the interval one improvement had been made on Leo's account by the great French cartographer D'Anville. Like his contemporary, Captain Cook, D'Anville took nothing on trust, nor did he care for the ornamental sports of the imaginations of early mapmakers. If there was any part of the world where the map was a blank inviting embellishment, it was Africa south of the Sahara, the part of the world of which Swift wrote:

> *So geographers, in Afric maps,*
> *With savage pictures fill their gaps,*
> *And o'er inhabitable downs*
> *Place elephants for want of towns.*

D'Anville belonged to the Age of Reason. He sifted the conflicting evidence about the course of the river and so became the first to distinguish between the Senegal and the Niger, though he remained vague about the ultimate course of the latter. On his 1749 map he noted: "All Nigritia, from the head of the Senegal, is very little known. I conclude that the Niger flows from West to East, and has no affinity with the Senegal or any Part thereof, but falls into some Lakes that communicate with the River Nile." It flowed through Wangara, "where the land is rich in gold; whereas the Senegal rises on the other side of the supposed mountains and flows west into the Sea." In fact, both rivers rise in the Futa Jallon range, one flowing to the east, the other to the west, as he supposed, but it needed Park's ocular evidence to confirm his hypothesis.

It was the uninviting, not to say lethal climate of West Africa which prevented the exploration of the interior that would set these problems at rest. Fever or dysentery killed off most of the early explorers, traders, missionaries, sailors engaged on the suppression of the slave trade, or soldiers on garrison duty. Service in those parts amounted to sentence of death and settlement in what came to be called the White

Man's Grave was out of the question. In 1825 the garrison at Jamestown at the mouth of the Gambia amounted to 108 men; four months later there were 21 survivors. Sierra Leone, established with difficulty as a home for liberated slaves, was "a pestiferous charnel house." The Gold Coast was "the most unfriendly to men of any country on the face of the globe." At Fernando Po the standing orders for the labour force were "Gang No 1 to be employed digging graves as usual. Gang No 2 making coffins until further notice." As for the Bight of Benin, it inspired the most sinister of sea chanties:

> *Beware and take care of the Bight of Benin,*
> *There's one comes out for forty goes in.*

The eighteenth century pathology of fevers was a strange jumble of frightening names, fallacious theories and futile remedies. Not knowing what caused Black Vomit (Yellow Fever) or Ague (Malaria), the doctors of those days had no idea how to prevent or cure them. Tropical medicine was naturally neglected by the profession at home, so that it was left to naval and army surgeons to make what observations and recommendations they could. Needless to say, they were ineffective. It seems strange to us that while they were continually complaining about being tortured by mosquitoes, not one of them connected the insect with the disease. This was because the pathology of the period was climatorial or, to use their word, "miasmatic." Everything was due to bad air or bad smells. Thus Dr Richard Mead, the leading expert on fevers, regarded the source of disease as contagion from the passage of unidentifiable poisons from one person to another. "It is propagated by three causes, the air, diseased persons, and goods transported from infected places" – such as stagnant pools, or "putrid exhalations from the earth," which he called comprehensively "miasmata." "Some authors have imagined infection may be conveyed by the means of insects, the eggs of which may be conveyed from place to place, and to make the disease where they are hatched. As this is a supposition grounded upon no matter of observation, I think there is no need to have recourse to it."

Surgeon Winterbottom, providing *Medical Directions for the Use of Navigators and Settlers in Hot Climates* in 1807, states that "the signs of an unhealthy country are great swarms of flies, mosquitoes etc., thick fogs lying on the ground for some time after sunrise, heavy dews, cold nights preceding very hot days" – a good description of the country through which the lower Niger passed. Dr John Wilson in 1846 tells the traveller that he may wander ashore with impunity during the day, "but let no man try it at night – death then, in the form of fever or miasm, lurks in every corner, hovers around every bush."

All fevers were regarded as basically the same, so that the very words *mal aria* indicate the pathology of the disease. That being so, treatment must be similar – phlebotomy or blood-letting on a murderous scale, calomel, laxatives, emetics to encourage "a gentle puke." Quack powders, such as the popular Dr James's Powder, were officially recommended. And, of course, there was Peruvian or Jesuit's Bark.

The efficacy of cinchona bark was a much debated topic. Dr James Lind, best known for his antidote to scurvy in the form of lemon juice (an effective prophylactic, which it took the Admiralty forty years to adopt), was also the author of the first treatise on tropical medicine in 1768. Though he followed Mead in the pathology of fevers, he had the good sense to provide practical suggestions on how to escape infection, which were all very well for naval persons but quite impracticable for explorers. Boat work in swamps or creeks, sleeping on shore, were to be avoided, but explorers could do nothing else. Lind was an effective propagandist for the use of bark rather than venesection as a cure and by 1808 naval surgeons were instructed to use it, but for some reason – whether the dosage was wrong, or whether it was exhibited in the wrong form – it fell out of favour just as the exploration of Africa began. Mungo Park was a surgeon, but he seems to have done nothing but take enormous doses of calomel which rendered him speechless for a week and let the fever run its course. The contents of Richard Lander's medicine chest are known, but it contained among its purgatives, emetics and stimulants only four oz. of sulphate of quinine, described as a "strengthener after fever or dysentery." No wonder that he died of fever, though by that date quinine had been isolated from cinchona bark and was manufactured by the Quaker chemists, Howards of Ilford. It appears in the London Pharmacopoeia and was sometimes used on board ship, but it was not favoured by a generation in which venesection enjoyed renewed popularity. Yet it was the use of quinine which proved to be the key to Africa, and it was Dr Baikie, a naval surgeon who was the last of our travellers, who proved beyond doubt its efficacy as a prophylactic on his Niger expedition in 1854. Thenceforward, as he prophesied, travel and settlement by the white man was feasible, provided care was taken to take quinine in wine regularly as a prophylactic and as a mitigant. Up to that time, as Captain Owen complained during his epoch-making survey of the African coastline in the twenties, "It may be questioned whether our very severe losses were not in a measure attributable to European medical practice, bleeding and calomel being decidedly the most deadly enemies in a tropical climate."

The barriers to a penetration of Africa were thus the difficulties of travel and communication, the absence of any overriding interest in the trade which it had to offer (apart from slaves) and the daunting reputation of its climate and its inhabitants. Why then, in the last decade of the eighteenth century, was such a concerted effort made to overcome such obstacles?

One reason, though not the most important, was the beginning of the campaign to abolish the slave trade. In 1783 the Quakers set up one of their formidable committees "for the discouragement of the Slave Trade on the coast of Africa." In 1785 Wilberforce met the converted slave captain John Newton, "the old African blasphemer," as he called himself, now a powerful preacher in the cause of abolition. Clarkson began to gather materials for his famous indictment of the trade and in 1788, with the support of Pitt and Fox, the first resolution was introduced into the House of Commons. But, as Wilberforce noted in his diary that year, "Called at Pitt's tonight. He firm about the African trade, though we begin to perceive more difficulties in the way than we hoped there would be." The West Indian interest was marshalling its opposition to the abolitionists. How the campaign fared is not our business here: suffice it to say that Africa was now news, so that the problems of the continent could no longer be ignored as they had been in the past.

More to the point was the shame felt in educated circles by representatives of the Enlightenment in England, Germany and France at the prevailing ignorance about so vast a continent. "Africa stands alone in a geographical view," exclaimed Major Rennell, the leading geographer of the day. "Penetrated by no inland sea, like the Mediterranean, Baltic or Hudson's Bay; nor overspread with extensive lakes, like those of North America; nor having, in common with other continents, rivers running from the centre to the extremities; but, on the contrary, its regions separated from each other by the least practicable of all boundaries, arid deserts of such formidable extent, as to threaten those who traverse them with the most horrible of all deaths, that arising from thirst! Placed in such circum-

25

stances, can we be surprised either at our ignorance of its interior parts, or of the tardy progress of civilization in it?"

The other great geographical mystery of the century – the extent of the Pacific and the nature of the Southern Continent – had just been triumphantly solved by Captain Cook. One is apt to forget that the man who, at the time, made the greatest reputation out of the first voyage was not Cook but Sir Joseph Banks, who, at the age of thirty-five, and largely as a consequence of that voyage, became President of the Royal Society for the next forty-two years. As an enthusiast for botany and natural history, as an organiser of geographical exploration, Banks stood pre-eminent in the world. If the blank on the map which was the Pacific had been filled, he felt that it was equally the duty of all "philosophers" (as scientists then called themselves) to fill the blank which remained in Africa. James Bruce, as a lone traveller, recently returned from Abyssinia, where he began the search for the sources of the Nile, had met Banks and was about to publish the narrative of his travels. In the person of the British Consul at Tangier, Banks had a protégé in James Matra, a midshipman on Cook's first voyage and a fellow enthusiast about settling New South Wales. The impending revolution in France was, of course, unrealised in England, where it seemed that the moment was propitious for transforming Banks's favourite dining club into the more serious African Association with a momentous resolution passed on June 9, 1788, at the St Albans Tavern, Pall Mall:

"That as no species of information is more ardently desired, or more generally useful, than that which improves the science of Geography; and as the vast Continent of Africa, notwithstanding the efforts of the Ancients, and the wishes of the Moderns, is still in a great measure unexplored, the Members of this Club do form themselves into an Association for Promoting the Discovery of the Inland Parts of that Quarter of the World."

2

Mungo Park's First Expedition

The twelve members of the Saturday's Club who thus found themselves transformed into a general staff for the organisation of African exploration consisted of the usual representatives of the Nobility and the Church – three dukes, eleven earls, four barons. There was the versatile Bishop of Llandaff, at one time Professor of both Chemistry and Divinity at the University of Cambridge. Their secretary was a Quaker wine merchant named Henry Beaufoy, to whom the prospectus of the African Association and its initial expansion were due. On his death he was succeeded by Bryan Edwards, best known today as the historian of Jamaica, who as a West Indian merchant did not share the abolitionist enthusiasm of some of his fellow members.

In his Plan of the Association Beaufoy pointed out that "almost the whole of Africa is unvisited and unknown," that the map of its interior was "still but a wide extended blank," and that "the source of the Niger, the places of its rise and termination, even its existence as a separate stream, are still undetermined." Since such ignorance was a reproach to science, he invited cultivated men, wherever their interest lay, to join the Association.

The committee which chose the new members was gratified by the response to this appeal. By 1790 there were 95 members. In 1810 there were 75, but in 1819, after the government had stepped in to sponsor official expeditions and after the death of Banks, its founder and tireless promoter, membership fell to 46, and in 1831, when the

Association was amalgamated with the new Geographical Society, there were only 14. Thereafter the Royal Geographical Society continued the work of the Association in promoting and supporting travellers in East Africa, such as David Livingstone; nearly all the expeditions to West Africa were sponsored by the government.

The size of the Association in its heyday shows how concerted was the effort to reach the Niger. Chief among its members was Major James Rennell. Though he was the leading geographer of the day, he perpetuated the legend that the Niger could never flow south because he exaggerated the size of the Futa Jallon range, where it rises, into a chain of mountains "of a stupendous height," variously called the Zong or Kong mountains, which stretched eastward parallel with the river's supposed course. There was also the cream of the intelligentsia of the age – Cavendish, Gibbon, Payne Knight, Dr Burney, John Hunter the surgeon, William Marsden the ethnologist who was also Secretary of the Admiralty, and the bankers Coutts and Hoare. Among the Quakers (always to be counted among subscribers to such an enterprise) there was Barclay the banker and Barclay the brewer, as well as Samuel Whitbread, brewer and politician. There was a strong group of Evangelicals – Lord Spencer, Lord Barham (both of them First Lords of the Admiralty), Thornton and Wilberforce. Among industrialists were Josiah Wedgwood (an enthusiastic abolitionist) and John Wilkinson, both with Quaker affinities.

The business of the Association was left in the hands of Banks, with Beaufoy as Secretary and Rennell as geographical adviser and part author of the annual Proceedings. Such was Beaufoy's enthusiasm that the Proceedings of 1790 read like a modern travel agent's brochure. Nowadays, he suggested, the traveller need not confine himself to the conventional visits of Grand Tourists to Naples; he could easily reach "the luxurious city of Tombuctoo, whose opulence and severe police attract the merchants of the most distant states of Africa; the mysterious Niger will disclose her unknown original and doubtful termination; and countries unveiled to ancient and modern research will become familiar to his view." According to him, the banks of the Niger were as densely populated as those of the Nile, but he forgot to mention the existence of the Sahara.

Who was to do the unveiling? The first candidates were not well chosen. One was Simon Lucas, Oriental Interpreter to the Court of St James, who claimed acquaintance with the Barbary states (Matra called him a born liar). He started out from Tripoli, but turned back after a hundred miles of desert without accomplishing anything.

The other was a foot-loose American who "felt an invincible desire to make himself acquainted with the unknown regions of the globe." His name was John Ledyard. He had shipped as a marine on Cook's last voyage and on his return to the United States had, strictly against orders, published an unofficial account of it. He then set out to *walk* across Russia in order to develop the fur trade on the Pacific coast. At Yakutsk, the coldest spot on earth in eastern Siberia, he was stopped by the Czarist police and unceremoniously dumped back on the Polish border. Thence, penniless, he turned up at the house of Sir Joseph Banks in Soho Square. Banks sent him to Beaufoy, who spread a map of Africa before him and traced a line from Cairo due west, which was the supposed direction of the westward flowing Niger. When would he be prepared to explore this route? "Tomorrow morning," replied Ledyard. "I have tramped the world under my feet, laughed at fear, derided danger. Through millions of savages, over parching deserts, the freezing north, the everlasting ice, and stormy seas have I passed without harm. How good is my God!" The enthusiastic young man was despatched to Cairo, where, after a few weeks, he died of a bad case of "Egyptian tummy".

Major Daniel Houghton was the next candidate, a fifty-year-old bankrupt Irishman, who evidently wanted to get away from his family. His chief qualification was that he only asked £300 for trade goods. The committee was impressed by his zeal, "the order of his mind and the strength of his constitution," so he was sent to attack the problem from the opposite direction, starting from the Gambia. How far he got remains uncertain. Having assumed Moorish dress and joined a caravan, he disappeared somewhere in the region of Bambara. As far as Mungo Park could learn, he was murdered by Moors at a spot which he was shown in that district.

"I am perfectly safe, and out of all danger," was the last message the Association received from him, though he added that the chiefs to the east were reputed to be less friendly. He was probably killed as a spy, though the conclusions which the Association drew was that he was murdered by robbers on account of the goods which he carried. Future travellers – and that meant Park – were therefore advised to take as little as possible with them. Before his disappearance, Houghton had made one important suggestion, if not discovery: that the Niger was distinct from the Gambia and the Senegal, and that it probably flowed east. It was left to his more fortunate successor to confirm this.

At the General Meeting of the Association on May 31, 1794, Beaufoy announced that the committee had agreed to employ Mr Mungo Park "as a Geographical Missionary . . . to ascertain the course and, if possible, the rise and termination of the River Niger, and that he shall use his utmost exertion to visit the principal Towns or Cities in its neighbourhood, particularly Tombuctoo and Houssa."

Mungo Park is possibly better known today for his

Christian name than for his achievements. Everyone knows that among his peers Cook stands for the Pacific and Livingstone for Africa, but only Scotsmen can explain the name which has given Park his immortality. Apparently it means "dearest" and is the alternative name for St Kentigern, the patron saint of Glasgow, who converted the Picts of Galloway.

He was born on September 10, 1771, at Foulshiels near Selkirk, the seventh child of a small farmer's family of thirteen. As a crofter's son, his upbringing was hard, so that he himself claimed that his chief qualifications as an explorer were his ardent desire "to become experimentally acquainted with the modes of life and character of the natives," his ability "to bear fatigue; and I relied on my youth and the strength of my constitution to preserve me from the effects of the climate."

He was intelligent, ambitious, tough and poor. He matriculated in anatomy and surgery at Edinburgh University, though he never proceeded to a degree in medicine. Like so many of his countrymen (Dr Lind, for instance, or Dr Baikie), the post of a ship's surgeon was the most suitable for a Scotsman of his modest qualifications and slender means. Moving to London, he lodged with his brother-in-law James Dickson, a gardener who was the friend of Banks. It was the latter who obtained for him a berth on board a ship belonging to the East India Company bound for Bencoolen, whence he returned to contribute a paper to the Linnaean Society on "Eight small fishes from the coast of Sumatra."

He was now twenty-three years old and, as events proved, rightly proud of the strength of his constitution and ambitious to "acquire a greater name than any ever did." He had the insatiable curiosity and invincible toughness of the true explorer, but hardly the intellectual equipment of a Cook or a Livingstone. He made little use of his scant qualifications in medicine during his travels. He had the barest knowledge of surveying, none of cartography, and no more than anyone else of the geography or peoples of the interior. Though he picked up the rudiments of the Mandingo language when he landed on the Unknown Continent, this was of no service to him beyond the region of the upper Gambia, so that he had to rely on interpreters. Nor had he ever travelled on land before. Because he was the only volunteer available, the Association chose him for a task which had already killed two other men. For 14/- a day, payable on his return, and £200 to cover his expenses, he was left to fend for himself. It was his own ability, patient courage, extraordinary capacity for survival and persistence on his quest which enabled him to achieve the fame which he so ardently desired.

He sailed for Africa without waiting for the badly-organised convoy which the authorities intended him to join, since Britain was now at war with Revolutionary France. Arriving at the mouth of the Gambia in June 1795, he made directly for the village of Pisania, which was the Africa Company's outpost some way up the river. Here the resident was Dr Laidley, to whom Beaufoy had written a letter of introduction. By the end of the month Park was down with his first bout of fever. Realising that he must await the end of the rainy season in August, he spent the time learning the local language, studying the habits of the natives and finding out what he could about the nature of the country ahead of him from the *slatees* or slave merchants coming from the interior.

The region through which he was to travel consists, for the most part, of monotonous rolling bush country, dotted with mud villages which were surrounded by patches of poorly cultivated land. To the northward lay the fringe of the desert, from which nomadic Moors (as Park always calls them) raided the cattle of the savannah country. To the

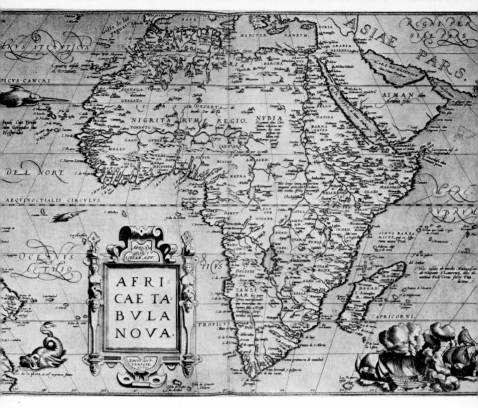

Africa by Abraham Ortelius, 1570, showing the Niger as an
extension of the combined Gambia and Senegal rivers.

Mungo Park:
a miniature
after Eldridge

(*Above*) Barbary and Nigritia by De L'Isle, 1700. The Gambia is now separated from the Senegal but the latter is still connected with the Niger

(*Left*) René Caillié meditating upon the Koran and taking notes

south, the extensive Futa Jallon range of hills provided the source of both the Senegal and the Gambia rivers flowing west, and the Niger flowing east. As they were only a few thousand feet high, the river meandered for hundreds of miles across a wide, barren basin to the north-east. As Park wrote, "The country, being an immense level, and very generally covered with woods, presents a tiresome and gloomy uniformity." The same was true of the diet of the inhabitants – meat, milk and the inevitable *couscous*, which he calls a "pudding."

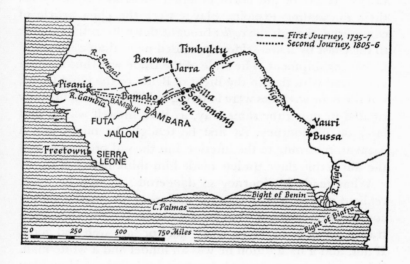

Because his route lay roughly along a latitude only 12° north of the equator, the heat of the day was such that a man could not walk barefoot or touch a rock without scorching his skin. The nights were cold, and the rains, which fell for the most part during the summer season, were tropical downpours which soaked a traveller in a few minutes. Park tells us that he set forth with an umbrella, but we hear no more of that useful appendage; later travellers found that it was the most popular of all gifts presented to African chieftains.

The inhabitants of the Senegambia area were Mandingos, Muslim negroes whose peaceable habits and love of academic arguments can have changed little from the date when Richard Jobson described them one hundred and fifty years earlier. Park says they were of "a mild, sociable and obliging disposition. The men are commonly above middle size, well shaped, strong, and capable of enduring great labour; the women are good-natured, sprightly and agreeable." The tawny Moors of the north despised them as easy prey for their marauding exploits. Slaves were the chief article of commerce, though the *coffles* brought down from the interior to the coast by *slatees* seldom provided more than a thousand a year for shipment. The scale of the trade was thus nothing compared with that in the Bight of Benin or the Gold Coast, but the poor wretches were fettered, half starved and brutally treated in much the same way, as Park himself was to find later on his journey. At first he thought he might join a caravan returning to the interior, but the sad procession and the unreliable slave traders made him think better of it.

What made his journey so dangerous, though he never realised it, was the fact that the natives of the interior simply could not understand what he was about. If a traveller was a trader, whether in slaves, ivory, gold or salt, well and good. If not, and if in addition he was an infidel and a white man, he must be a spy. As such he must be killed, as Houghton had been, or at least humiliated. When, as in Park's case, he carried little to rob and was obviously defenceless, his presence in the fanatical Muslim lands further north was a provocation to murder.

Mungo Park set out on his journey on December 2, 1795. With him he had a Mandingo servant and interpreter called Johnson, who had once been shipped as a slave to the West Indies, and a boy called Demba, "a sprightly youth," who

34

was promised his freedom when he returned. There were four other negroes, two of them *slatees*, in the little caravan. Park provided himself with a horse, two donkeys, and an assortment of beads and tobacco as currency; "a few changes of linen, an umbrella, a pocket sextant, a magnetic compass and a thermometer; two fowling pieces and two pairs of pistols." Never was a traveller more modestly provided for. No wonder neither he nor Dr Laidley ever thought to see each other again.

"I had before me a boundless forest, and a country, the inhabitants of which were strangers to civilised life, and to most of whom a white man was the object of curiosity or plunder. I reflected that I had parted with the last European I might probably behold, and perhaps quitted for ever the comforts of Christian society." He was just twenty-four years old.

As he made his obligatory visits to the "kings" of each district he was regularly warned that those further east were of a more hostile disposition. At the entrance to each village he noticed the masks and costumes of witch doctors, "which I was told belonged to MUMBO JUMBO." On arrival – such was the custom of the country – he stood about waiting for an invitation to lodge with one of the inhabitants. For the first part of his journey, this was regularly forthcoming; only later, when he was in rags, indifference or open hostility was his fate.

From the territory of the Mandingos and the upper waters of the Gambia and the Senegal rivers he passed into Bondou, part of the territory of the Fulani (whom he called Foulahs), whose loosely-knit empire extended far to the east beyond Timbuktu to the Hausa states. They were pastoral in habit and more strictly Muslim in religion, often thievish and fanatical, but not so cruel as the Tuareg tribes of the desert to the north, the veiled people who lived by banditry or blackmail. Park describes the Fulani as "of a tawny complexion, with small features and soft, silky hair . . . they evidently considered all the Negro natives as their inferiors, and always rank themselves with white people."

The change in the character of the people was brought home to him when he encountered his first bandits on Christmas Day. They pretended to be representatives of the king of Joag, claiming that he had entered the king's territory without paying the accustomed dues.

"I had indeed entered without knowing that I was to pay the duties beforehand, but I was ready to pay them now, which I thought was all they could reasonably demand. I then tendered them, as a present to the king, the five drachms of gold which the king of Bondow had given me; this they accepted, but insisted on examining my baggage, which I opposed in vain. The bundles were opened, but the men were much disappointed in not finding in them so much gold and amber as they expected. They made up the deficiency, however, by taking whatever things they fancied; and after wrangling and debating with me till sunset, they departed, having first robbed me of half my goods. These proceedings dispirited my people, and our fortitude was not strengthened by a very indifferent supper after a long fast. . . . Towards evening, as I was sitting upon the Bentang, chewing straws, an old female slave passing by with a basket upon her head, asked me *if I had had my dinner*. As I thought she only laughed at me, I gave her no answer; but my boy, who was sitting close by, answered for me, and told her that the king's people had robbed me of all my money. On hearing this, the old woman, with a look of unaffected benevolence, immediately took the basket from her head and showing me that it contained groundnuts, asked me if I could eat them; being answered in the affirmative, she presented me with a few handfuls, and walked away before I had time to thank her for this seasonable supply. This trifling circumstance gave me peculiar satisfaction. I reflected with pleasure on the conduct of this poor untutored slave who, without examining into my character or circumstances, listened implicitly to the dictates of her own heart."

Such was to be his experience as he travelled further east into the interior. At each town his baggage was searched and rifled, either by Moors or by the local tribesmen, but at each place negroes helped him when they could. "Whatever difference there is between Negro and European in the confrontation of the nose and the colour of the skin, there is none in the genuine sympathies and characteristic feelings of our common nature."

Rumours of war between the Kaarta people of the north and the army of Mansong, king of Bambara to the south, with the sight of numerous refugees, further depressed him. He thus describes a typical Moorish raid.

"About two o'clock, as I was lying asleep upon a bullock's hide behind the door of the hut, I was awakened by the screams of women and a general clamour and confusion among the inhabitants. At first I suspected that the Bambarrans had actually entered the town; but observing my boy on the top of one of the huts, I called to him to know what was the matter. He informed me that the Moors were come a second time to steal the cattle, and that they were now close to the town. I mounted the roof of the hut and observed a large herd of bullocks coming towards the town, followed by five Moors on horseback, who drove the cattle forward with their muskets. When they had reached the walls, which are close to the town, the Moors selected from the herd sixteen of the finest beasts, and drove them off at full gallop. During this transaction the townspeople, to the number of five hundred, stood collected close to the walls of the town; and when the Moors drove the cattle away, though they passed within pistol shot of them, the inhabitants scarcely made a show of resistance."

It was essential to press on before the spring rains. On

February 18, 1796, he passed the village from which Major Houghton had sent his last letter and was shown the place near Jarra in the district called Ludomar where he was either murdered or died of hunger.

At Deena on the borders of Bambara his companions refused to accompany him any further after another Moorish attack. "They assembled round the hut of the negro where I lodged and treated me with the greatest insolence. They hissed, shouted and abused me; they even spat in my face with a view to irritate me and afford a pretext for seizing my baggage. But finding such insults had not the desired effect, they had recourse to a final and decisive argument, that I was a Christian, and of course my property was lawful plunder to the followers of Mahomet. They accordingly opened my bundles and robbed me of everything they fancied. My attendants, finding that everyone could rob me with impunity, insisted on returning to Jarra. . . . I resolved to proceed alone. It was moonlight; but the roaring of wild beasts made it necessary to proceed with caution."

It was a mistake to proceed north of Jarra because it led him into the country of a tyrant called Ali. The boy Demba ran after him, and soon after Johnson was brought along by a band which had captured him. But at Benown Ali compelled him to undress, asked him to eat a wild hog and when he refused to be so insulted, ordered the boys to beat the hog and the women to plague the Christian: "I was a *stranger*, I was *unprotected*, and I was a *Christian*: each of these circumstances is sufficient to drive every spark of humanity from the heart of a Moor."

For a month he was held captive, Ali refusing him permission either to continue his journey or to return to Jarra. Suffering from thirst, he was denied the use of a cup and compelled to kneel with the cattle to drink out of their trough. The heat, the hunger and thirst, the continuous insults would have broken a lesser man, but somehow he controlled himself sufficiently to avoid giving mortal offence. He never seems to have used his firearms: perhaps because these would have been the first article to be stolen. He even preserved a sense of humour. When the natives demanded a personal inspection to find out if circumcision was a European custom, he agreed, provided he was left alone with the prettiest girl in the crowd. "The ladies enjoyed the jest, and went away laughing heartily; and the young damsel herself seemed in no way displeased at the compliment, for she soon afterwards sent me some meal and milk for my supper."

With the arrival of Queen Fatima (who lived up to her name and complained that Park's long red beard was too good for a Christian), he was at last permitted to return south to Jarra with his two attendants. At the last minute Ali changed his mind and retained the boy, at which Park was so angry that he confessed he would have murdered him. He succeeded in making arrangements for Demba's redemption from slavery, only to be informed by Johnson that he himself would go no further. So Park again continued on his way alone, driving his horse before him because the animal was too weak to carry him. All that he now possessed was two shirts, two pairs of trousers, two handkerchiefs, an upper and under waistcoat and a pair of boots. The theft of his cloak, which he wrapped round himself at night, was a final insult on the part of Moorish bandits.

At last he was free of the land of thieves and murderers, but he had no money, no food and no companions. After fainting from exhaustion, he struggled on to a village where an old, motherly-looking negress, squatting at the door of her hut, took pity on him and revived him with a dish of *couscous*. A few days later he entered a belt of cultivated land and saw the smoke of Segu, the capital of Bambara, rising in the distance. It was a large walled town built on both banks of the Niger (here called the Joliba), forming a surprising prospect of civilisation which he had not expected to find in this part of Africa.

Having joined a small caravan, as he and his fellow travellers approached the town on July 20, one of them called out "See the water! And looking forwards, I saw with infinite pleasure the grand object of my mission – the long sought for majestic Niger, glittering to the morning sun, as broad as the Thames at Westminster, and flowing slowly *to the eastward*. I hastened to the brink and, having drunk of the water, lifted up my fervent thanks in prayer to the Great Ruler of all things, for having thus far crowned my endeavours with success."

To his mortification, he could find no lodgings, the inhabitants of towns being less hospitable than those of villages. At length, once more, another kindly old woman allowed him to sleep in her hut, for which he paid her two of the four brass buttons remaining on his waistcoat, the only recompense he could make.

Mansong, king of Segu, was anxious to get this red-headed infidel out of his dominions as soon as possible. He gave him some cowries, the currency of the interior, and hastened him on his way down the Niger towards Jenne. Timbuktu was still "the great object of my search," but when he heard that it was inhabited by "savage and merciless people, who allow no Christian to live there," he had to think again if he was to avoid another spell of captivity. At the large town of Sansanding he could not understand a word that was said to him and now he had no interpreter. He had to abandon his horse, now too feeble to walk, far less carry his master: "I surveyed the poor animal, as he lay panting on the ground, with sympathetic emotion; for I could not suppress the sad apprehension that I should myself in a short time lie down and perish in the same manner of fatigue and hunger."

When he reached the town of Silla, two days short of Jenne, on July 29, "worn down by sickness, exhausted with hunger and fatigue, half naked, and without any article of value by which I might procure provisions, clothes, or lodging," he decided to turn back. Timbuktu was obviously beyond his reach, but he had achieved the chief object of his journey by establishing the eastward course of the Niger. He made every effort to discover its course beyond Timbuktu, but no one he spoke to had the slightest idea of what happened to the river beyond that point – some, indeed, were convinced that it flowed "to the end of the world."

So the five-hundred-mile journey back to the coast began. He decided to return by a route lying south of his former one. Though the terrain was equally difficult, it lay through Bambara and not through a region constantly raided by Moors from the desert. Some of the inhabitants proved surly towards this ragged stranger as he limped through their villages, others were more kindly. As if by a miracle, as he was passing through a village near which he had abandoned his horse and thrown away the saddle, he heard a horse neighing and recognised it as his own. So the two wretched figures, man and horse, continued slowly and painfully on their way westward, swimming creeks, climbing long stony hills, fearing attacks by lions or robbers, shivering from fever. At one point he thought it was all over with him. Having caught up with some sinister looking figures travelling in the same direction,

"one of them said in the Mandingo language, 'This will do' and immediately snatched my hat from my head. Though I was by no means free of apprehension, yet I resolved to show as few signs of fear as possible, and therefore told them that unless my hat was returned to me, I should proceed no further. But before I had time to receive an answer, another drew his knife and seizing upon a metal button upon my waistcoat, cut it off and put it in his pocket. Their intentions were now obvious and I thought that the easier they were permitted to rob me of everything, the less I had to fear. I therefore allowed them to search my pockets without resistance and examine every part of my apparel with the most scrupulous exactness. Even my half-boots (though the sole of one of them was tied on to my foot with a broken bridle rein) were minutely inspected. Whilst they were examining the plunder, I begged them, with great earnestness, to return my pocket compass; but when I pointed it out to them, as it was lying on the ground, one of the banditti, thinking I was about to take it up, cocked his musket and swore that he would lay me dead on the spot if I presumed to put my hand upon it. After this, some of them went away with my horse and the remainder stood considering whether they should leave me quite naked, or allow me something to shelter me from the sun. Humanity at last prevailed; they returned me the worst of the two shirts, and a pair of trousers; and as they went away, one of them threw back my hat, in the crown of which I kept my memorandums; and this was probably the reason why they did not wish to keep it. After they were gone, I sat for some time looking around me with amazement and terror. I saw myself in the midst of a vast wilderness in the depth of the rainy season, naked and alone; surrounded by savage animals and men still more savage. I was five hundred miles from the nearest European settlements. All these circumstances crowded at once on my recollection; and I confess my spirits began to fail me. I considered my fate as certain, and I had no alternative but to lie down and perish.

"The influence of religion, however, supported me. . . . At this moment, painful as my reflections were, the extraordinary beauty of a small moss, in fructification, irresistibly caught my eye. I mention this to show from what trifling circumstances the mind will sometimes derive consolation; for though the whole plant was not larger than the top of one of my fingers, I could not contemplate the delicate conformation of its roots, leaves and capsula without admiration.

Can that Being (thought I) who planted, watered and brought to perfection, in this obscure part of the world, a thing which appears of so small importance, look with unconcern upon the situation and sufferings of creatures formed in His own image? – surely not! I started up, and disregarding both hunger and fatigue, travelled forwards, assured that relief was at hand; and I was not disappointed."

Soon afterwards he fell in with a slave dealer who was collecting a *coffle* of slaves to take down to the coast. This man, named Kafra, took pity on him and gave him some clothes. Kafra remained his benefactor to the end. As soon as the rains were over, a sad procession began its journey to the Gambia. The slaves, says Park, "are commonly secured by putting the right leg of one and the left of another into the same pair of fetters. By supporting the fetters with a string, they can walk, though slowly. Every four slaves are likewise fastened together by the necks with a strong rope of twisted thongs; and in the night an additional pair of fetters is put on their hands, and sometimes a light iron chain passed round their necks." In this *coffle*, however, they moved more freely, so that they could do twenty to thirty miles a day.

Their march began on April 19, the party consisting of thirty-five slaves for sale and fourteen free men or domestic slaves. Those who could not keep up with the rate of march were whipped, or in the case of two women who ate clay in order to commit suicide, abandoned. Their track led them through the Jallonka wilderness, where villages burned by the Fulani increased the desolation of the scene. It was a toilsome journey for all. Slave and free alike were footsore, blistered by the sun and in some cases literally stung to death by bees. Having crossed the branches of the upper Senegal they at last rejoined Park's outward route near the head-waters of the Gambia after a march lasting nearly two months.

Park parted from the *coffle* near his destination, Pisania.

"Although I was approaching the end of my toilsome and tedious journey, and expected in another day to meet with countrymen and friends, I could not part, for the last time, with my unfortunate fellow travellers, doomed, as I knew most of them to be, to a life of captivity and slavery, in a foreign land, without great emotion. During a wearisome peregrination of more than five hundred British miles, exposed to the burning rays of a tropical sun, these poor slaves, amidst their own infinitely greater sufferings, would commiserate with mine; and frequently of their own accord, bring water to quench my thirst, and at night collect branches and leaves to prepare me a bed in the wilderness. We parted with reciprocal expressions of regret and benediction. My good wishes and prayers were all I could bestow upon them, and it afforded me some consolation to be told that they were sensible I had no more to give." Though, as this passage shows, Park could not be blind to the sufferings of slaves, he was in no real sense an abolitionist. No more were his employers, who sent him out as "a geographical missionary" and a naturalist, not as an agent for the extinction of slavery or even the abolition of the trade, which in any case was at that date still perfectly legitimate.

On June 11, 1797, he re-entered the village of Pisania and soon afterwards met Dr Laidley once more, who welcomed him "as one risen from the dead." Kafra was paid twice the amount he had been promised and arrangements were even made to expedite the sale of his slaves, for there were few vessels on the coast at the time. Freshly clothed, his beard shaven off (which turned him from a man to a boy, said Kafra), his mind and body at rest, Park continued down the river to take a passage as a surgeon in an American slaver bound for Carolina, the only vessel available. She carried 130 slaves, of whom eleven died on the voyage because of their close confinement rather than from exceptional ill usage: "the mode of confining and securing Negroes in the

American slave ships (owing chiefly to the weakness of their crews) being abundantly more rigid and severe than in British vessels employed in the same traffic, made these poor creatures suffer greatly, and a general sickness prevailed amongst them."

The vessel was a leaky old hulk, soon to be condemned as unseaworthy, so that she was forced to alter course to Antigua in the West Indies. Here Park managed to get a passage on board a packet bound for Falmouth, arriving on December 22, 1797, after an absence of two years and seven months.

3

The Death of Mungo Park

Sir Joseph Banks's encomium on Park's return was as magisterial as befitted the President of the Royal Society and of the African Association: "Strength to make exertions, Constitution to endure fatigue, and Temper to bear insults with Patience, Courage to undertake hazardous enterprises when practicable, and Judgement to set limits to his exertions when his difficulties were likely to become insurmountable."

The narrative of Mungo Park's travels, when it became available to the general public, bore out this testimony to his character. The notes of the journal, which he had kept carefully hidden in the crown of his hat through all his adventures, were first put in order for the benefit of members of the Association by its new Secretary, Bryan Edwards, with geographical notes by Major Rennell. Park was then permitted to write them up himself for the general public, with Edwards keeping an eye on his style because the young man had little practice in such work. When the book appeared in 1799 it was a triumphant success, nor has it ever subsequently been out of print. For the first edition of 1500 copies the author received the princely sum of a thousand guineas. Three further editions rapidly sold out. With his accumulated salary from the Association, Park must have been a rich man when he returned to his native Scotland.

His book has always had a popular appeal because it is a short sober account of extraordinary events. The incidents described were sufficiently dramatic in themselves to make elaboration unnecessary; nor was he the sort of man capable of throwing a romantic colouring over his adventures, because he was temperamentally incapable of padding out the story with verbose descriptions. "It has nothing to recommend it but *truth*," he declares in the preface; "it is a plain unvarnished tale." As such, the narrative has always had a wide public, though the author's attitude towards slavery did not make him a friend of the abolitionists, who were now in full cry. He accepted the African scene as he saw it. He had himself endured the hardships and humiliations inflicted on slaves, but he realised that slavery was a trade and a custom so deeply rooted in African society that there was nothing to be done about it beyond pressing for the abolition of the European trade. Nor, during his brief appearance in London society, did he make much of an impression. Unlike the majestic figure of his predecessor in Africa, James Bruce, he was a silent and aloof figure in the salons of lion-hunters because of a natural shyness in such society.

Back in Scotland, he married Ailie Anderson, the daughter of a Selkirk surgeon. From his letters to her we can see how deeply he was capable of emotional response, a side of his character seldom apparent in the bare prose of his narrative. But his adventures had spoiled him for the life of a country doctor. Explorers are by nature restless people, so that even after the hardships which he had endured, and which continued to haunt his dreams, nothing could deter him from further activity. "Tired of a life of indolence," he set up in practice at Peebles, but soon found it "a laborious employment, and I will gladly hang up the lancet and plaister ladle whenever I can obtain a more eligible situation." He would rather face all the horrors of Africa, he told Sir Walter Scott, than wear out his life riding over the hills of Scotland, "for which the remuneration was hardly enough to keep body and soul together."

He therefore lent a willing ear to Banks's suggestion for

further employment. The first proposal was the exploration of the hinterland of New South Wales, in which Banks of course took a special interest. Having agreed to go, Park backed out because of the enormous separation which a voyage to New Holland (as it was still called) would entail in his family life. The Niger problem was now being attacked from the north by such explorers as Hornemann, and Rennell was propounding further fallacious theories about its easterly course. He was convinced that the river terminated in lakes in Central Africa because of his obsession about the height of the mountains of Kong. When he was told that there were Arabs who thought that it terminated in the sea, he insisted that this was a misunderstanding of the meaning of the word *bahr*, which he thought was applicable to lakes as well as sea.

Banks kept the problem alive by stressing its political rather than its geographical issues. If Napoleon had sent ships to reconnoitre Australia, if he himself had landed in Egypt, why should he not send an expedition inland from French Senegal? Sir Joseph informed the Colonial Secretary that there was in existence a book "written with the clear intention to induce the French to colonize the whole of the Senegambian country." After the British seized Goree at the mouth of the Senegal, the government began to show an interest in anticipating such an imperialist move. A wild scheme was propounded by a Colonel Stevenson to raise a black regiment in the West Indies and sent it to Timbuktu, with the assistance of Canadians who were to build canoes for the force. Park was to lead an advance party of 150 men from the African Regiment, which was to be "augmented by as many Volunteers as may offer from the Hulks and public Prisons."

Park himself was invited by Lord Hobart on behalf of the government "to take another trip into the centre of Africa to discover the termination of the Niger," and Banks advised

North Africa by D'Anville, 1749, (detail).

D'Anville's map of 1749 was the first to distinguish between the Senegal and the Niger, here shown flowing east past Tombut (Timbuctoo) and Ghana (Kano). A novel feature is the river flowing south via Lamlen, on which is marked Bussa on the middle Niger. D'Anville concludes his note on Nigritia, still "little known", with the observation: "There are reasons to presume that the Niger, which gives the name to this country, flows from west to east, contrary to the usual opinion on the subject."

Sir Joseph Banks
by Sir Thomas Lawrence

Two Musicians: from Denham, Clapperton and Oudney
Travels in Northern Africa 1828

him to return to London to await developments. However, Addington's government fell and with it the grandiose proposal to invade Africa, but Lord Camden's appointment as Colonial Secretary in Pitt's new government led to another invitation in 1804 to submit plans for an expedition.

Considering Park's experience, they were not good plans. They were clearly influenced by the absurd military schemes, and their lack of realism is surprising. His judgement may have been warped by a subconscious desire for revenge for all the insults to which he had been compelled to submit. Geographical and scientific considerations now took a secondary place. It seems that he was now determined to employ sufficient force to prevent him falling a second time into the hands of the Moors and if necessary to shoot his way through to his objective.

For this purpose he said he required a force of thirty European soldiers, twenty negro servants, fifty asses, six horses and six carpenters to build a boat at Segu in order to sail down the river. He must have known that, in wartime, such men could only be recruited from the dregs of the army and navy. He was told to find the carpenters through the Agent for Convicts at Portsmouth dockyard and in this way obtained four such men out of the hulks. At Goree, the garrison of the Royal African Corps was "composed of deserters and persons confined on board the Hulks who desired, on being pardoned, to serve His Majesty abroad." No wonder that on his arrival there they volunteered with remarkable enthusiasm: anything to escape from the climate of Goree. No wonder that a certain Lieutenant Edward Martyn, aged twenty, agreed to command them if he, too, could avoid garrison duty at such a place. The inexplicable thing is that Park accepted such recruits so willingly for an expedition which, no one knew better, required extremes of courage and endurance.

The scale and manning of the expedition was all wrong

and its ultimate route remained necessarily vague. If, as Rennell argued, the Niger ended in lakes, Park could not return upstream and it seemed too dangerous to proceed across the desert to the north or east; "the only remaining route that holds out any hopes of success is that towards the Bight of Guinea" – in accordance with his own theory that the Niger was connected in some way with the Congo, the argument being that the former was a river with a beginning but no known end, while the latter was a river with an end but no beginning.

Neither Banks nor Rennell were happy about these proposals. The latter was annoyed at Park's Congo theory, which had been suggested to him by an old African trader. Banks was dismayed at the risks entailed, though he reluctantly accepted them. "I am aware," he told the Colonial Secretary, "that Mr Park's expedition is one of the most hazardous a man can undertake, but I cannot agree with those who think it too hazardous to be attempted. We are wholly ignorant of the country between the Niger and the Congo and can explore it only by incurring the most frightful hazards."

The least worried person seemed to be Park himself. He secured the appointments of his brother-in-law, Alexander Anderson, as second-in-command, and of another fellow countryman, George Scott, as artist or draughtsman; but there was nothing he could do to hasten the loading of stores and he knew that the dry season was ending. Nevertheless, he sailed quite happily from Portsmouth on January 31, 1805. At Goree he met Lieutenant Martyn and his party of thirty-five soldiers, together with two sailors who volunteered to rig and navigate "our Nigritian man of war." It was strange that they should be so doing just about the time the battle of Trafalgar was fought. Though he knew that the rains must soon break, he pressed on up the Gambia with his heterogeneous caravan of red-coated soldiers, horses and donkeys, surely the most extraordinary collection of men that any explorer has ever commanded.

Among the few Africans who accompanied him there was one exceptional Mandingo, who was hired as a guide. Isaaco, as he was called, proved to be the most loyal and efficient member of the expedition, and it is to him that we owe our knowledge of the final tragedy. As Park never returned, the account of his second journey is in the form of the disconnected notes composing his journal. These were sent back to the coast by Isaaco, who much later gathered from the sole survivor the story of the subsequent events which occurred in his absence.

The caravan set out from Pisania on May 4, the order of march being Isaaco and George Scott at the head of the column, Lieutenant Martyn in the centre, with Anderson and Park bringing up the rear. Within a few days the rains broke and the column began to disintegrate. Park's letters continue to be optimistic until June 10, when the first despondent entry appears in his journal after a particularly heavy storm: "The tornado had an instant effect on the health of the soldiers, and proved to us to be *the beginning of sorrow*. I had flattered myself that we should reach the Niger with a very moderate loss . . . but now the rain had set in, and I trembled to think that we were only half way through our journey. . . . June 13. Very uneasy about our situation: half of the people being either sick of the fever or unable to use great exertion, and fatigued in driving the asses."

His route lay to the south of his return route on his previous expedition. He was keeping as far away from the Moors as possible until he reached the Niger, but the stony tracks and numerous creeks which they had to cross made the going difficult. In spite of the fact that Park himself was suffering from fever, he was continually rounding up stragglers or reloading the asses when their burdens overturned. The carpenters were the first to be left behind, but soon one soldier after another dropped out, overcome by the heat or enfeebled by fever. All night their sleep was disturbed by the roaring of lions or the bellowing of hippos. At one point they nearly lost Isaaco, who was attacked by a crocodile when wading across a river. With great presence of mind, he thrust his finger into the eye of the beast and yelled for a knife to cut himself free. The crocodile's jaws closed on his thigh and even after he had freed himself attacked a second time, pulling him under water, until again he thrust his thumb into its eye. Park ends the record of that day with the words: "Found myself very sick, and unable to stand without feeling a tendency to faint; the people so sickly that it was with some difficulty we got the loads put into the tents, though it threatened to rain."

Pilfering on the part of the natives and retaliatory shooting on the part of the soldiers began some time before they reached the Niger. Stragglers and deserters disappeared in the bush, while the sick, who had to be abandoned, were accommodated with payment at friendly villages. Park mentions in particular a Scottish soldier, who was "of a naturally cheerful disposition, who used to beguile the watches of the night with songs of our dear native land." Anderson was so bad that Park had to carry him on his back across streams, while two soldiers carried him in a hammock on the march.

On August 19 they reached the Niger at Bamako in the country of Bambara: "I went on a little before, and coming to the brow of the hill, *I once more saw the Niger* rolling its immense stream along the plain." Of the thirty-eight Europeans who set out from Goree, only seven reached the river. The facts hardly warrant the conclusion which Park drew at this stage of his journey that up to now he had been on friendly terms with the inhabitants and that "with common prudence any quantity of merchandise may be transported from the Gambia to the Niger without danger of being robbed by the natives." It was fortunate that this rash prediction was never put to the test.

As soon as possible one of the big canoes which navigated the river was hired to carry them downstream at a rate of five knots. Though he was dosing himself against dysentery with so much calomel that he could neither eat nor sleep for a week, Park's optimism revived at the sight of the river and at what seemed such a painless way of travel. "We travelled pleasantly all day; in fact nothing can be more beautiful than the views of this immense river; sometimes as smooth as a mirror, at other times sweeping us along at the rate of six or seven miles per hour."

Soon they were met by the emissaries of King Mansong of Segu, who told them that once again the king refused to meet him (he seems to have thought that Park was some kind of magician) and, as before, was to be hurried out of his territory with the gift of cowries. Making his own gifts on a generous scale, Park took the opportunity of asking for a canoe to sail down the Joliba "to the place where it mixes with salt water." The king was so relieved that he promised him two canoes and a free pass as far as Timbuktu.

The final embarkation took place at Sansanding, east of Segu. It was a large city with two mosques and a thriving market. As there was the usual delay about the delivery of the canoes, Park opened a stall in the market in order to earn enough money to buy one. Consumers flocked to his exotic collection of goods, thereby earning him the jealousy of other traders, who were as anxious as the king to see him gone.

When the royal canoe at last arrived it was found to be half rotten. Isaaco was sent back with more presents – two blunderbusses, two fowling pieces, two pairs of pistols and five muskets which would not fire – to ask for another. He returned with one forty foot long, six foot broad, flat bottomed so that it drew only a foot of water, and stoutly built for the most part. However, it took Park and one of the soldiers eighteen days to repair other parts of it before it could be launched on the river as His Majesty's Schooner *Joliba*. An awning of bullock hide was rigged to protect the crew from any spears or missiles thrown at them from the banks; muskets and pistols were laid ready at hand to repel boarders; a large supply of provisions was taken on board; and all was prepared to make a dash down the river, wherever it led, without stopping on the way.

Before Park sailed, however, another tragedy occurred which seems to have made him desperate to conclude his ill-fated expedition. On October 28 Anderson, the only surviving European apart from the impetuous young Martyn and three soldiers (one of whom was crazed), died of fever after a long illness. "No event which took place during the journey ever threw the smallest gloom over my mind, till I laid Mr Anderson in the grave," wrote his brother-in-law. "I then felt myself as if left a second time lonely and friendless amidst the wilds of Africa."

He intended to sail on November 16, because his journal ends with the words: "All ready and we sail tomorrow morning, or evening." But since his last letter home is dated Sansanding, November 19, there must have been some hitch. Fortunately, the natives were friendly. As he wrote to a friend, "Whitbread's beer is nothing to what we get at this place, as I feel by my head this morning, having been drinking all night with a Moor." Martyn was also of the party, at which he says he "got a little tipsy – finished the scene by giving the Moor a damned good thrashing." An earlier letter by this trigger-happy young man shows what a dangerous companion Park had to rely on, now that Anderson was dead and Isaaco sent back to the coast. "Thunder, Death and Lightning – the Devil to pay: lost by disease Mr Scott, two sailors, four carpenters and thirty-one members of the Royal African Corps, which reduces our numbers to seven, out of which Dr Anderson and two of the soldiers are quite useless, the former from one disease or another has been for four months disabled; we every day suppose he'll kick it. . . . Excellent living since we came here, the Beef and Mutton as good as was ever eat. Whitbread's beer is nothing to what we get here."

Park's last letters informed Banks and his wife that with the five survivors he intended to sail as soon as he sealed them and despatched them back to the coast with Isaaco: "I do not intend to stop or land anywhere till we reach the coast, which I suppose will be some time in the end of January. . . . You may be sure that I feel happy at turning my face towards home." Nothing further was ever heard from him. His true epitaph occurs in his last letter to the Colonial Secretary: "Though all the Europeans who are with me should die, and though I myself were half-dead, I would still persevere; and if I could not succeed in the object of my journey, I should at least die on the Niger."

The story of the events which took place during the next few weeks must be pieced together from information obtained by Isaaco five years later. When Park failed to return (even the exact date of his death is unknown), and rumours of a catastrophe began to fly about in the strangest places – Bombay (from a pilgrim to Mecca), Ethiopia, Morocco – the Governor of the Gambia sent Isaaco back to the Niger to find out what had happened. He had the extraordinary luck to meet Amadi Fatuma, Park's guide down the river, at Sansanding, whose first words were: "They are all dead; they are lost for ever." The story which Amadi told him five years after the event was confirmed in outline by later European travellers.

HMS *Joliba*, a big enough boat to carry a hundred men, sailed with only five Europeans (Park, Martyn and three soldiers), and three African slaves, with Amadi as guide, on board. They had fifteen muskets between them and to avoid trouble with the inhabitants, who Park rightly regarded as fanatical Muslims, only Amadi was occasionally sent on shore to purchase milk and vegetables. Off the port of Timbuktu (they never saw the city itself) they repelled the first attempt to impede their rapid progress downstream. Further on they beat off an attack by seven canoes, on one occasion, by twenty on another. Any attempt to make contact with the huge canoe was met with musket fire, until Amadi tried to restrain Martyn, who seems to have been the chief culprit, with the words "Martyn, let us cease firing; for we have killed too many already." Martyn would have killed him too for his interference, had not Park intervened.

There may have been some excuse for Park's policy of a dash down river, because the country was in an unsettled state and on several occasions they saw armed bands (which Amadi called armies) – Tuareg in the Timbuktu region, Fulani further round the great bend of the river – gathered on the banks; but it meant that much offence was taken by the chiefs of the towns past which they swept. These strangers did not pay the customary tolls, nor did they even ask permission to continue their journey. Word was passed from one village to another, warning those further down the river of the arrival of Park's canoe. It seems that by such means he was finally trapped where the mile-wide river narrowed at some rapids.

At Yauri, the first of the Hausa towns visited after rounding the three-hundred-mile bend of the river, Amadi was sent on shore, because it was here that his contract to serve Park ended. He was immediately imprisoned by the king, who was furious at what he regarded as Park's inadequate gifts. According to Amadi, the king sent an armed band to intercept the canoe at the rapids of Bussa, fifty miles south, where some rocks formed a sort of bridge under which the boat must pass. It is more likely that he advised the king of Bussa to ambush the white men there, because there was no time even for horsemen to reach the spot, so swift was the canoe's progress. The excuse later offered by the people of Bussa was that they mistook Park's men for scouts of an invading army.

Amadi's informant, the one slave who survived the wreck, described the final tragedy in these words:

"There is before this village a rock across the whole breadth of the river. One part of the rock is very high; there is a large opening in that rock in the form of a door, which is the only passage for the water to pass through; the tide current is here very strong. The army went and took possession of the top of this opening. Mr Park came there after the army had posted itself; he nevertheless attempted to pass. The people began to attack him, throwing lances, pikes, arrows and stones. Mr Park defended himself for a long time; two of his slaves at the stern of the canoe were killed; they threw everything they had in the canoe into the river, and kept firing; but being overpowered by numbers and fatigue, and unable to keep the canoe against the current, and no probability of escaping, Mr Park took hold of one of the white men and jumped into the water; Martyn did the same, and they were drowned in the stream in attempting to escape. The only slave remaining in the boat, seeing the natives persisting in throwing weapons at the canoe, stood up and said to them, 'Stop throwing now, you see nothing in the canoe, and nobody but myself, therefore cease. Take me and the canoe, but do not kill me.' "

None of this was known in England for five years. The first news came from the British consul at Mogador in 1810, who heard it from a Moorish trader. Even then Park's wife refused to believe her husband was dead and her son went out to the Gold Coast to search for him, but was never heard of again. The first confirmation of the slave's story came in 1826, when a Tuareg attacked Gordon Laing in the middle of the Sahara, claiming that it was he who had shot and wounded him at Bussa twenty years before. (See below, page 68.) "How imprudent, how unthinking! I may say how selfish it was in Park," Laing told a friend, "to attempt to make discoveries in this country at the expense of the blood of its inhabitants, and to the exclusion of all after communication. How unjustifiable was such conduct!"

Since Laing himself was murdered by such men shortly afterwards, the comment is ironic. Other explorers were more generous to the memory of the young Scotsman. That same year Hugh Clapperton and his servant, Richard Lander, arrived at Bussa from the south to make enquiries. Clapperton found the inhabitants strangely unwilling to speak of the affair. It had all happened a long time ago, when they were boys, but there remained a sense of guilt in the air. Clapperton told the king that he wanted nothing but any books or papers which might have survived, "and that with his permission I would go and visit the spot where they were lost. He said no, I must not go; it was a very bad place."

After his master's death, Lander on his return south was detained at Wawa, where he was given some muskets to clean. These, he found, had the mark of the Tower armoury on them and were clearly part of the official issue to the soldiers. When in 1830 he returned to Bussa with his brother to embark on his historic voyage down the Niger, he saw a sporting gun and an embroidered robe which Park had given to the previous king. He also saw a nautical almanac, but was unable to bring any of these things back with him.

In 1857, however, Lieutenant Glover (see below, page 200) was able to purchase the almanac, which he presented to the Royal Geographical Society, in whose archives it is still preserved. This, together with a silver-topped walking stick now used as the staff of office by the Emir of Yauri, remain the only relics of Mungo Park.

The memory of this red-bearded stranger, firing so desperately from his fast moving boat, haunted the inhabitants of the villages along the great bend of the river. Fifty years later Heinrich Barth, the first traveller to explore that stretch of the Niger in detail, heard stories of his fate which "proved what an immense excitement the mysterious appearance of this European traveller, in his solitary boat, had caused among all the surrounding tribes."

4

The Attack from the North

The attack on the Niger problem from the north began in 1797, when Friedrich Hornemann, a Göttingen theological student, offered his services to the African Association. Accepting them principally because of his fine physique and obvious enthusiasm, he was asked to carry out the plan which had failed when Ledyard, the first of the explorers, had died at Cairo nine years earlier.

Hornemann arrived in Egypt only a few weeks before Bonaparte invaded the country, but the latter supported his plan to travel west, even though after his own experience of the Bedouin on his march from Alexandria he considered that the young German was mad.

Disguised as an Arab merchant, Hornemann crossed the desert with a caravan as far as Tripoli and Murzuk, the capital of the Fezzan district to the south, which was the last place from which any news was received from him. In his broken English he informed Banks: "I leaved Tripoli on 1 December 1799 and arrived here at the Capital of Fezzan January 20, 1860 [sic] after a long but happy Travel. I am in the best health in few words very well." His last letter, dated April 6, added that he was going south to Bornu, "being very healthsome and perfectly acclimated to this country."

No one knows what happened to him after that. It seems probable that he made an extraordinary journey to Bornu and beyond it to within a day's journey of Rabba, on the lower Niger, where he died of dysentery. No news of his fate was heard for seventeen years and since he left no journals of any kind, his heroic journey was fruitless. He was not the only young adventurer to be lost without trace in Central Africa.

The first news about him was brought back by Lieutenant G. F. Lyon, RN, in 1818, the only survivor of a party of three men led by Major Ritchie who travelled south with a caravan from Tripoli. Ritchie and the other man died at Murzuk, but Lyon, after proceeding a little further, turned back to publish a narrative of the expedition. It is an unremarkable book, except for its brilliantly coloured aquatints of desert life and some appalling glimpses of the Arab slave trade. They themselves had to join a slave raiding expedition as the only means of travel along a route marked by the bones of those who failed to reach the slave market. At Tripoli, says Lyon, a negress fetched £20 if she was in good condition, whereas in the desert the sale of a horse would purchase twenty of them.

Ritchie had none of the attributes of an explorer and seems to have squandered the resources of the expedition before he died, leaving the young naval officer with no option but to return. Lyon, on the other hand, had convivial habits of mixing with the natives to dance and drink *booza*, a heady potion made from millet. In this way he picked up rumours, if not information, about the course of the Niger. "All agree," he wrote, "that by one route or other these waters join the great Nile of Egypt." When John Barrow reviewed his book in the *Quarterly Review*, he seized upon this, the only nugget of geographical information brought back by Lyon, as confirmation of the prevailing view of the easterly course of the river.

During the Napoleonic wars there had been a long interval when no further efforts were made to discover the Niger and the activity of the African Association was (except for Park) suspended. After 1815, however, the search was renewed, largely owing to the enthusiasm and influence of John Barrow, who now superseded the ageing Banks as the principal organiser of exploration. He was Second Secretary of the Admiralty, John Wilson Croker being the First, or as we should say, Parliamentary Secretary. Barrow made his name as a traveller and writer when he accompanied Lord Macartney's embassy to China before the war. He had then gone to South Africa as Macartney's secretary, where he travelled extensively and wrote a widely read book about the new Cape Colony which earned him the reputation of an African expert, a reputation which made him somewhat opinionated about a continent of which he really knew only a small part. He was a man of immense industry, occupying a very influential position, so that his passion for extending geographical knowledge – whether in Africa (where he worked behind the scenes, since overland exploration was the business of the Colonial Office), or in Arctic exploration (where he renewed the search for the North West Passage) – gave the necessary impetus for a new age of discovery.

Now that the war was over there was an opportunity for employing naval ships and officers in the advancement of science, for which reason so many of the Niger explorers were naval officers. But it is typical of the haphazard way in which exploration was organised at that time that no sooner had Lyon returned from the scorching sands of the Sahara than he was sent to freeze on the second of the new attempts to find an Arctic passage. Nor did Barrow content himself with sending officers on such expeditions: he often wrote up their journals for them, arranged to have them published by his friend John Murray and even reviewed the results in the *Quarterly*, to which he was an assiduous contributor for over forty years. As a member of the Council of the Royal Society, and as the founder of the Royal Geographical Society, Sir John Barrow (as he became) did indeed inherit the mantle of Sir Joseph Banks.

"To what purpose could a portion of our naval force be, at any time, but more especially in time of profound peace, more honourably or more usefully employed than in completing those details of geographical and hydrographical science of which the grand outlines have been boldly and broadly sketched by Cook, Vancouver and Flinders, and others of our countrymen?"

So Barrow wrote in the introduction to Captain Tuckey's posthumous account of a voyage to the Congo in 1816. It was a tragic voyage which illustrates the fixed ideas which permeated Barrow's thinking about the Niger. Either, as Lyon later convinced him, the Niger flowed into the Nile; or, as Park suggested earlier, it formed part of the upper waters of the Congo. The real explanation, which was first suggested in 1802, Barrow dismissed out of hand: "The hypothesis of Mr Reichard, a German geographer of some eminence, which makes the Niger pour its waters into the gulf of Benin, is entitled to very little attention" – merely because Reichard had never been there.

In order to test the Congo theory, Captain James Kingston Tuckey was sent. Why he was chosen remains a mystery because, apart from carrying out the first survey of Sydney harbour and occupying his leisure in a prison camp by composing four unreadable volumes on maritime geography, poor Tuckey had no qualifications whatever. He suffered from a serious liver complaint and he had never travelled in the tropics before.

Barrow's instructions for this voyage to the Congo (then called the Zair, a name which has now been revived for political reasons) illustrate the extraordinary ignorance about Central Africa which prevailed even after the travels of Mungo Park:

"That a river of such magnitude as the Zair should not be known with any degree of certainty beyond 200 miles from its mouth is incompatible with the present advanced state of geographical science, and little creditable to those Europeans who, for three centuries nearly, have occupied various parts of the coast near to which it empties itself into the sea. . . . If in your progress it will be found that the general trending of its course is from the north-east, it will strengthen the conjecture of that branch and the Niger being one and the same river. . . . It is also probable that a very considerable branch of the Zair will be found to proceed from the east or south-east, as it has been ascertained that all the rivers of Southern Africa, as far as the division of the continent has been traversed from the Cape of Good Hope northwards, flow from the elevated lands on the eastern coast across the continent, in a direction from west to north-west; and it may perhaps be considered as a corroboration of the existence of some easy water communication between the eastern and western coasts of South Africa, that the language of Mozambique very nearly resembles the language spoken on the banks of the Zair. . . . In all your proceedings you are to be particularly mindful of the health of the officers and men under your orders."

According to Barrow, the expedition sailed with every chance of success. The vessels chosen were the *Dorothea* storeship and the *Congo* steamship, the first of its kind ever to be employed in the Navy. However, her paddles and 20 h.p. engine had to be removed during her trials at Greenwich, so that she sailed as a conventional sloop of war. At the mouth of the Congo the *Dorothea* was sent home (she appeared next year on an Arctic expedition), leaving HMS *Congo* to work her way two hundred miles up river until her progress was checked at the first rapids. By that time Tuckey and most of his officers were dead, so that she sailed home in the charge of the master and the surgeon. Thus, Barrow comments somewhat ineptly, "by a fatality that is almost inexplicable, never were the results of an expedition more melancholy and disastrous." The explanation was perfectly simple, had

Barrow known as much about the climate of West Africa as
he did about that of South Africa. The Congo had to wait
fifty years for her explorer in the person of H. M. Stanley
after the key to African exploration had been discovered in
the use of quinine on the later Niger voyages.

Tuckey's was the first of three almost contemporaneous
attacks of the Niger problem, the other two being an
expedition from the Gambia and the Ritchie–Lyon expedition from Tripoli. The first of these was another pathetic
failure because it was a repetition of all the worst features of
Park's last expedition – a force of over a hundred troops, only
a handful of whom ever reached the upper Niger. It was
commanded by Major John Peddie of the 12th Foot, who
died before reaching the borders of Senegal, as did his
successor, so that the remnant was led back to the coast by
Major William Gray. Meanwhile Surgeon Dochard took a
sergeant and seven men as far as Segu in 1818 before turning
back; Dochard died soon afterwards. Except for a meeting
with Park's old guide, Isaaco, the expedition contributed
nothing to the geographical knowledge of the area.

The impetus of the attack from the north by Lyon and his
successors must be attributed to Barrow. It happened that in
1817 a naval survey officer, W. H. Smyth (better known
today as the compiler of an excellent nautical dictionary and,
with Barrow, the founder of the Royal Geographical Society)
in the course of his work at Malta had occasion to visit the
friendly Bashaw of Tripoli. The latter had decided to
present the Prince Regent with some columns from the
Roman ruins at Leptis Magna, columns which now stand in
a romantic Claudean setting at Virginia Water in Surrey.
After his visit Smyth wrote to his admiral:

"I am becoming still more convinced that here, through
this place, and by means of this people, is an open gate into
the interior of Africa. By striking due south from Tripoli, a
traveller will reach Bornu before he is out of Yusuf's (the

Bashaw) influence; and wherever his power reaches, the protecting virtues of the British flag are well known. In fact, looking at the unavoidable causes of death along the malarious banks of the rivers of the western coast, I think this ought to be the chosen route, because practicable into the very heart of the most benighted quarter of the globe."

The admiral forwarded the letter to the Secretary of the Admiralty and Barrow persuaded the Colonial Office to launch the Ritchie–Lyon expedition because, as he told Banks, "We shall not perhaps be able to find another Lord Bathurst at home, or another Bashaw of Tripoli, so favourable for the undertaking."

The reason for the Bashaw's friendliness may be connected with Lord Exmouth's bombardment of Algiers the previous year. Exasperated by the continual depredations of the Barbary corsairs, an Anglo–Dutch fleet put the port out of action for the time and freed hundreds of white slaves imprisoned in the city. The lesson was not lost on Tripoli, where the Bashaw Yusuf played off the English against the French with great skill for many years. At this period British influence predominated in the person of the consul, Hanmer Warrington, a genial and hospitable figure who was a good friend to all the northern explorers. It was from his villa just outside the city (a *résidence somptueuse*, according to his jealous French rival) that, with the Bashaw's permission, Ritchie and Lyon, Denham and Clapperton, and the young Gordon Laing all joined caravans on their way south. Many did not return, the saddest loss of all being Laing who had fallen in love with Warrington's daughter. The consul married them, but refused to permit them to consummate the union until Laing's return, a cruel decision which reveals another aspect of Warrington's character. As well as being a domestic tyrant, his despatches home show him a conceited bore who tried to take all the credit for the discoveries of the younger men who went south.

The story of the Denham–Clapperton expedition may be postponed to the next chapter, partly because by its success it differed from the abortive attempts chronicled in this chapter, partly because in Hugh Clapperton appeared one of the major figures in African exploration. Gordon Laing's appointment to follow them, though by a different route, was made before Clapperton's return to England, though Warrington was able to inform him of the important news from the Sultan of Sokoto that the Niger flowed south. Laing, a conceited young man with an obsession about Timbuktu, was determined to forestall Clapperton or anyone else in the discovery of the river.

Gordon Laing began life as a lieutenant in the Royal African Corps at Sierra Leone. He was not popular with his superiors, because he had a mind of his own and an arrogance of manner which must have made him a difficult man in the mess. He travelled in the country behind Sierra Leone and published a book about it. He then had the effrontery to appeal over the heads of senior officers direct to the Commander-in-Chief at the Horse Guards, demanding promotion. He also wrote direct to Lord Bathurst, volunteering to complete the work of his countryman, Mungo Park. The offer would have been turned down, had not Barrow persuaded the Colonial Secretary to let him try.

Even before he set out from Tripoli in 1825, Laing had made an important contribution to the study of the river. While travelling near its source in the Futa Jallon hills, he noted that the altitude of the source could not be sufficient to carry the waters as far as Egypt: "The question of the Niger uniting with the Nile must therefore be ever at rest." It says much for Barrow's patience that he encouraged a man who thus arrogantly disposed of his favourite theory.

Two caravan routes of great antiquity led south from Tripoli, along which negro slaves and gold dust from Wangara had reached the Mediterranean for many hundreds of years. One was the Roman Garamantine Way to Murzuk in the Fezzan and thence across the Sahara to Bornu and Lake Chad. This was the route taken by Hornemann, Denham and Clapperton. The other was via the Ghadames oasis to the west, a far more dangerous route to Timbuktu because it ran through those parts of the desert which were haunted by the marauding Tuareg tribes. This was to be Laing's route, and he was the only Christian in an Arab caravan.

Soon after he started he was told about Clapperton's news concerning the probable course of the Niger. It was typical of Laing's self-confidence that he told a friend that he had already guessed as much before he left England: "The information of Sultan Bello now, in my opinion, sets the matter entirely at rest, or as nearly so as can be until the river is absolutely navigated to its *embouchure*, but I rather apprehend that it will not satisfy Mr Barrow, who is determined that the Yeou or Schad shall be the Niger." When Warrington cheerfully suggested that he might look forward to meeting Clapperton on the river, now that the latter was going to try to reach it from the south, Laing replied: "Clapperton may as well have stayed at home, if the termination of the Niger is his object – It is destined for me – It is due to me, and neither a Pearce [Clapperton's companion] nor a Clapperton can interfere with me – Tombuctoo shall be visited, and the Niger explored within a very few months."

Nor was Park exempt from Laing's criticism in pursuance of his own ambitions. Soon after his caravan entered Tuareg territory, Laing was accosted by an old man, who swore that he was Park and that it was he who had wounded him a long time ago.

"When you consider that the great discrepancy in point of time (I being only 31 years of age, and the expedition of Park having taken place twenty-one years ago) is a matter of no moment among people who do not trouble themselves with investigation, you will regret it as much as I do now, absurd and ridiculous as it may at first appear, for I cannot view without some apprehension the difficulties in which it may involve me in my attempts at research hereafter on the great artery of this unexplored continent."

It was not this old grudge but plain brigandage which precipitated the tragedy of Gordon Laing. Warrington heard the news from an Arab servant. Some hundred miles short of Timbuktu, Laing was set upon in his tent at night. He was wounded with sabre cuts on his head and thigh and his arm was broken. In spite of these terrible wounds, he was taken on to Timbuktu, "the far-famed capital of Central Africa," as he loved to call it. There he was imprisoned and tormented in one of the miserable mud huts which composed the city. He never realised that he had arrived in the middle of a bitter struggle for the town between the Tuareg and the Fulani. In spite of his wounds and his guard, he managed to slip out to see the Niger itself at the port a few miles outside the town. In his last letter to Warrington he told him that "my destination is Segu, whither I hope to arrive in fifteen days, but I regret to say that the road is a vile one, but my trust is in God Who has hitherto borne me up amidst the severest trials."

Two days after he had been permitted to begin his journey he was again set upon by fanatical tribesmen and murdered, apparently because he refused to turn Muslim. His papers were destroyed, so that apart from a few personal letters nothing remains for him to be remembered by. The editor of what he left has called him "the most neglected of the great explorers."

Some light on the fate of this rash young man was cast soon after the event by the most attractive of these lone adventurers – René Caillié, a young Frenchman who, like Laing, was obsessed by the ambition to reach Timbuktu.

While still at school, he recalled, the city was the subject of all his thoughts, so that he became resolved to reach it or perish. In 1824 the French Geographical Society offered a prize of 2000 francs to the first man to visit the town. In 1828 Caillié returned to Paris to claim the reward, though (as Barrow promptly and patriotically informed the French) Gordon Laing was actually the first European for many centuries to reach this fabled place.

Caillié lived in a humble capacity in French Senegal, though it is not clear what his exact position was. He trained himself for his chosen aim by travels in the hinterland until, in 1827, he set off up the valley of the river Nuñez (somewhat south of Sierra Leone) to cross the unexplored stretch of country between those parts and the upper Niger. The disguise he assumed was that of a Muslim pilgrim who had been captured as a boy by Europeans and was now returning from (alternatively, proceeding to) Mecca. It seems incredible that no one penetrated his disguise as an Arab during all the hardships which he underwent, and that pious Muslims gave the *hadji* food and alms at almost every stage of his route. His Arabic must have been astonishingly fluent, and he took care to be properly assiduous in his religious observances: there is a delightful illustration in his book subtitled "Mr Caillié meditating upon the Koran and taking notes." Even when he was reduced to the humiliating role of a beggar, he continued making notes "in haste and trepidation", for "I carried always in my leather wallet a sentence of death, and how often was that wallet necessarily confided to the hands of enemies."

During the first part of his journey through a negro pagan land, where sinister secret societies of witch doctors abounded and pious Muslims were few, he paid his way with trade goods. He had invested the capital saved from his wages in goods which were easily portable – knives, scissors, mirrors, tobacco, amber, cloves – and good friends had provided him

with a few medicines, including a small quantity of sulphate
of quinine; but his most valuable possession, since he
travelled unarmed, was an umbrella. As with Park and
Lander, this served not only to protect him from sun and
rain, but as an object to be greatly admired by negroes, who
were fascinated by the way it opened and shut.

He was never one for elaborate scenic descriptions, though
his accounts of the villages through which he passed and the
way of life of their inhabitants are admirable. The first part
of his journey as he travelled north-east through the foothills
of the Futa Jallon range does not concern us here. Suffice it
to say that all went well until he reached the Bambara
country bordering on the upper Niger. Here, at a place
called Timé, he was forced to stop for over six weeks owing
to a severe attack of scurvy. Now that his trade goods were
almost exhausted, he could buy no food and just as he was
about to complete the last stage of his journey to the Niger
he went lame and developed the dreaded symptoms of a
disease which struck all travellers, whether by sea or land,
who suffered from malnutrition.

"Violent pains in my jaw informed me that I was attacked
by scurvy, and I soon experienced all the horrors of that
dreadful disease: the roof of my mouth became quite bare, a
part of the bones exfoliated and fell away, and my teeth
seemed ready to drop out of their sockets. I feared that my
brain would be affected by the agonizing pains I felt in my
head, and I was more than a fortnight without sleep. To
crown my misery, the sore in my foot broke out afresh, and
all hope of my departure vanished. The horror of my
situation may be more easily imagined than described –
alone, in the interior of a wild country, stretched on the
damp ground, with no pillow but my leather bag which
contained all my luggage, with no medicine and no attendant
but Baba's old mother. . . . At length, after six weeks of
indescribable suffering, during which time I subsisted solely

on boiled rice and water, I began to feel better and to reflect on what was passing around me. I scarcely ever saw Baba. I could easily perceive that I was a trouble to him and his family, and that they were tired of the burthen of a man who was continually ill. The presents which I had been obliged to make them every now and then were rapidly exhausting my means, and my baggage was becoming so scanty that I feared I should not have sufficient merchandise to complete my journey; for, ill as I was, I did not now renounce the idea of continuing it. I would rather have died upon the road than have returned without making more important discoveries."

Although a local wise-woman was sent to cure him with some pieces of a red wood boiled in water as a mouth wash, he experienced little relief until nature herself cured him to the extent of allowing him to venture out, with the aid of a stick, from the noisome hut where he had been immured for so long. Then his luck changed. He was able to accompany a merchant to Jenne, which he reached at the end of the year, and embarked on the mighty Niger for Timbuktu towards the end of March, 1828.

He took a passage in one of the large canoes which made regular voyages downstream laden with food supplies for the city, because the soil round Timbuktu was too poor for local agriculture. Flotillas of up to eighty small canoes, similarly laden, were to be seen making the same voyage, but his own boat was a big one of about sixty tons burthen, 100' long, manned by fifty slaves and possessing a half-deck built on to the crazily-constructed hull. The planks were caulked with a mash of straw and bound together with cords. As pumps were unknown, there was always six inches of water in the bilge, in spite of the fact that a dozen slaves with large calabashes were constantly employed baling out the water. Sometimes the deck crew rowed the clumsy vessel along, sometimes they landed to tow her. Sometimes they punted her, with the master standing in the stern using a long pole as a rudder.

On 20 April they reached the port of Timbuktu, the city itself lying some eight miles away from the river.

"At length we arrived safely at Timbuctoo, just as the sun was touching the horizon. I now saw this capital of the Soudan to reach which had so long been the object of my wishes. On entering this mysterious city, which is an object of curiosity and research to the civilised nations of Europe, I experienced an indescribable satisfaction. I never before felt a similar emotion and my transport was extreme. I was obliged, however, to restrain my feelings, and to God alone did I confide my joy. This duty being ended, I looked around and found that the sight before me did not answer my expectations. I had formed a totally different idea of the grandeur and wealth of Timbuctoo. The city presented, at first view, nothing but a mass of ill-looking houses, built of earth. Nothing was to be seen in all directions but immense plains of quicksand of a yellowish white colour. The sky was a pale red as far as the horizon: all nature wore a dreary aspect and the most profound silence prevailed; not even the warbling of a bird was to be heard. . . . The heat was oppressive, not a breath of air freshened the atmosphere. In the whole course of my travels I never found myself more uncomfortable. . . . The city of Timbuctoo forms a sort of triangle, measuring about three miles in circuit. The houses are large, but not high, consisting entirely of a ground floor. In some, a sort of little closet is constructed above the entrance. They are built of brick of a round form, rolled in the hands and baked in the sun. This mysterious city, which has been an object of curiosity for so many ages, and of whose population, civilization and trade with the Soudan such exaggerated notions have prevailed, is situated in an immense plain of white sand, having no vegetation but stunted trees and shrubs. It may contain at most about ten or twelve thousand inhabitants; all are engaged in trade. The population is at times augmented by the Arabs, who come with the caravans and remain awhile in the city. Though one of the largest cities I have seen in Africa, it possesses no other resource but its trade in salt, the soil being totally unfit for cultivation. The inhabitants procure from Jenne everything requisite for the supply of their wants."

At first he was surprised at the inactivity of a place which was the chief market for salt in the western Soudan, but he soon discovered the reason. The place was virtually surrounded by bands of Tuareg horsemen from the desert, who held the city and its inhabitants to ransom. Occasionally, one of these brigands would gallop into the streets on a magnificent horse, tether it to a hut pole and demand food and drink and money from the occupant. At other times large bands would descend upon the city with similar demands. The negro inhabitants – the Moorish merchants being for the most part visitors – invariably paid up without making any resistance.

Since the Moors did not welcome strangers, Caillié was apprehensive, in spite of his disguise, when he found himself quartered in a house opposite that which Gordon Laing had been given the previous year. However, he was accepted as an Arab and regaled with descriptions how the foreigner had been baited as an infidel before he was murdered.

"Often, when seated before my door, I thought of the fate of that unfortunate traveller, who, after surmounting numberless dangers and privations, was cruelly assassinated when on the eve of returning to his own country. I could not repress a feeling of apprehension, lest, should I be discovered, I might be doomed to a fate more horrible than death – to slavery!"

His informants told him with relish how "one of the murderers tied a turban round the neck of his victim and strangled him on the spot, he pulling one end while his comrade held the other. The corpse of the unfortunate Laing was cast upon the desert, to become the prey of the raven and the vulture, the only birds which inhabit those desolate regions." He was even shown Laing's pocket sextant, but dared not purchase it. After being shown the spot outside the town where the murder took place, "I averted my eyes from this scene of horror, and secretly dropped a tear – the only tribute I could make to this ill-fated traveller, to whose memory no monument will ever be reared on the spot where he perished." In 1910, however, the French authorities exhumed two skeletons there, one of a European adult and the other of an Arab boy. They were reburied at Timbuktu.

Caillié, of course, made discreet enquiries about the course of the great river. All agreed that it flowed east to the land of the Haussa and emptied itself in the Nile; but, as he adds in a footnote, "the word 'Nile' is generic, as are also the terms 'Bahr'Ba', 'Kourara' and many similar names." He was told that the river near the city was called "Dhioliba" (Joliba), but not that the middle Niger was called the Quorra. "The great problem of the issue of the Dhioliba into the ocean will thus be left to the demonstration of some more fortunate traveller; but, if I may be permitted to hazard an opinion as to the course of the river, I should say that it probably empties itself by several mouths into the Gulf of Benin."

It was an intelligent guess, because Caillié had probably never heard of Reichard's hypothesis, and it was not till two years later that Lander (who knew nothing of the Frenchman's travels) proved its truth.

After two months at Timbuktu, Caillié continued his journey – as Laing had hoped to do – in the company of a caravan of Moorish merchants. They were an exceedingly unpleasant lot, showing him none of the courtesy of the Muslims in the city. On the journey across the harsh desert of the Berbers to Fez in Morocco, young Caillié suffered all the privations and indignities of a mendicant; but he survived. He made his way to Tangier, where he got in touch with the French consul in circumstances of the utmost secrecy. So good was his disguise, so brown his skin, so tattered his clothing, the consul refused at first to believe that he was a French citizen. In the end he was smuggled on board a ship bound for Marseilles. René Caillié got back to Paris to claim the prize for the first traveller to reach Timbuktu. After three years of incredible hardships, no one was better entitled to it, and the book which he wrote describing his journey is one of the most enthralling narratives of travel ever written.

5

Hugh Clapperton

If one were to describe what was officially called the Mission to Bornu from materials published by the participants, the result would be both tedious and misleading. The *Narrative of Travels and Discoveries in Northern and Central Africa in the years 1822, 1823 and 1824, by Major Denham, Captain Clapperton and the late Doctor Oudney,* which appeared in 1826, was written by Denham with the purpose of arrogating to himself all the credit for the expedition. The last section was, indeed, a Journal of an Excursion to Soccatoo, written by Clapperton, because he alone went there; but his previous discovery of the river Shari south of Lake Chad was deliberately suppressed by Denham, the names of his companions were only mentioned incidentally, in spite of the fact that this was supposed to be the account of a joint expedition, and the section would not have appeared at all, had not Barrow insisted. Until a few years ago, when the late E. W. Bovill printed for the Hakluyt Society the full correspondence of the travellers, no one realised what an unhappy drama of personal relationships was played out under the burning sun of central Africa.

It was due to Warrington at Tripoli and Barrow in London that another expedition to attack the Niger problem from the north was planned soon after the return of Lieutenant Lyon. They were encouraged to do so when the Bashaw offered an armed escort of a thousand men, provided the British government paid him £5000. That his writ did not extend across the desert, and that the offer was a mere pretext to extort money from the British government, seems to have escaped the consul's notice.

The first man to volunteer was a retired naval surgeon, aged thirty-two, named Walter Oudney, an unassuming little man now in private practice at Edinburgh. Barrow warned him against the attempt because he suffered from tuberculosis, and Oudney himself seems to have had a pre-monition of his death before he started; but he was convinced that a warm climate was his only hope, and the fact that he was a trained naturalist led the Colonial Office to accept his offer.

As a companion, Oudney suggested a neighbour called Hugh Clapperton, a tall solidly-built lieutenant in the Royal Navy, now on half-pay, who had served in the East Indies. "My friend Lieutenant Clapperton," he told Barrow, "is a gentleman of excellent disposition, strong constitution and most temperate habits, who is exceedingly desirous of accompanying the expedition. He wishes no salary, his sole object being love of knowledge." Since he was a naval officer on half-pay, Barrow persuaded the Colonial Office to give him £100. His service record, both in the East Indies and in Canada, proved him to be a man of courage and hardihood. Had the two companions alone been sent, the story of the expedition would have been happier and more fruitful.

At the last moment, however, Major Dixon Denham wrote from the Military College at Sandhurst to offer his services. After a conversation with Lieutenant Lyon, he drew up an ambitious plan for a march south to "the Niger or the Nile of the Negroes." It may be that the fact that he required no salary decided the matter for the authorities, but the consequence was that the chain of command was never clearly decided: Oudney imagined that he was the senior officer; Denham regarded him as a mere naturalist and assumed the same authority; so that Clapperton was forced into a subordinate role which he never intended when he volunteered. It is not surprising that a clash of personalities subsequently recurred which strongly recalls the more celebrated quarrel between Burton and Speke during their search for the sources of the Nile a generation later. Moreover, their instructions were drawn up in so slipshod a manner that Clapperton is called Shakleton and Oudney is told in one place that he is not to consider Denham as under his orders, but in another refers to "the expedition placed under your command."

In the geographical section of the instructions the hand of Barrow is again clearly visible: "The main object of your Journey is to explore the Country to the Southward and Eastward of Bornou, principally with a view to tracing the course of the Niger and ascertaining its Embouchure." The aim reflects his conviction that if they discovered a great Lake they would find the Niger passing through it. When the party did indeed reach Lake Chad, Denham lost all interest in the river, so that it was left to Clapperton to find out what he could by travelling westward rather than eastward. Why the two men separated will appear from the events which took place on the shores of Lake Chad, their one major discovery.

Oudney and Clapperton reached Tripoli in the autumn of 1821. At Warrington's house they met a young wastrel called John Tyrwhitt, who was to be appointed consul in the interior merely because his father wanted him out of England on account of the debts that he had run up. At one point of the expedition he was recalled on the grounds of ill health, but later rejoined it and died before the consular matter was settled. Consuls were strange appointments in those days, but the claims of young Tyrwhitt to become His Majesty's representative in central Africa seem to be the most curious of all.

A sturdier companion who joined them there was William Hillman, an almost illiterate shipwright from Malta, who

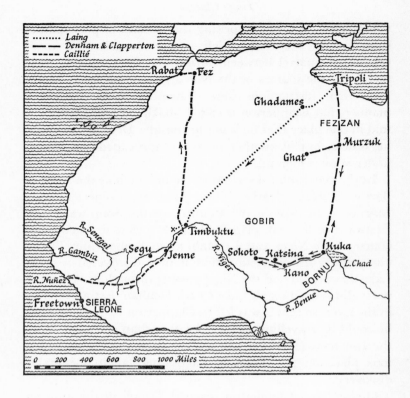

was to prove the most reliable member of the party. Denham himself joined in his own good time. But it was not until March, 1822, that the Bashaw's force was ready to set out and by that time Oudney and Clapperton had gone ahead to Murzuk.

Even by then there was friction between the three men. The Scotsmen naturally regarded Denham as an interloper, nor did the vanity of this Byronic-looking soldier allay their resentment. For his part, Denham told his brother,

"In the choice of my companions, I do not think H.M. Government have shewn their usual sagacity: we are not well classed and I have scarcely a fair chance. They are both

Scotchmen and as one of them [Clapperton] is under my orders and the Consul, Dr Oudney and myself independent of each other, no small jealousy exists on their part, and to push me off the stage altogether would be exactly what they wish. My Lieutenant's conduct has been such here on the road and at Tripoli that had I reported it, he must have been broke or at least sent home, so vulgar, conceited and quarrelsome a person I scarcely ever met with. The Dr (who is almost Dominie Sampson with more cunning), this son of War, or rather of Bluster, completely rules; therefore any proposition coming from me is generally negatived by a majority."

The Sheikh of Murzuk, capital of the Fezzan, welcomed the travellers with sherbet and coffee in a style quite different to the reception of the lonely explorers who had ventured into Africa hitherto. Accompanied as they were by a force of cavalry, he had little choice. He advised them to continue as they were like Christians, and not attempt to disguise themselves as Hornemann had done so many years before. Murzuk was a town of ill repute among Europeans, so that when the travellers were lodged in the same house where Ritchie had recently died, their spirits fell. And when the Sheikh casually informed them that there was no intention of proceeding south at this time of year, Denham threw up the sponge. He hastily retreated to Tripoli, whence, after a stormy interview with Warrington, he made his way to Marseilles. There the consul informed him that the Bashaw had changed his mind and would now send another escort to Bornu. He at once returned, choosing to interpret his flight as a means of forcing the Bashaw to do what was required. The Colonial Office, however, did not see that matter in the same light and he was told to act in future "with more circumspection."

The reaction of his companions, so suddenly deserted at Murzuk, may be imagined. "He has left without instructions of any description," Clapperton complained to Barrow; "neither has he written to the Dr – however his absence will be no loss to the mission and a saving to his country, for Major Denham could not read his sextant, knew not a star in heaven and could not take the altitude of the sun." "For my part," wrote Oudney, "I have never borne so much from any man as from him, and all for the sake of Peace. Had I known the man, I would have refused my appointment, and allowed some other to reap the honour attached to it. But it is now too late and what I have undertaken I hope to accomplish with credit to my Country and myself."

The two friends made a short excursion to Ghat some miles to the westward, chiefly to get away from unhealthy Murzuk. When Denham rejoined them in November he confesses his surprise that no one came out to meet him. The explanation was that all three Europeans were confined to their beds with fever and "nothing could be more disheartening than their appearance."

On the march south across seven hundred miles of desert the party consisted of the four white men, a negro servant called Columbus, a Gibraltar Jew as storekeeper, and several merchants wishing to take advantage of the escort. The next sixty-eight days were tough going, a beautiful watercolour of a small oasis by Clapperton showing one of the few spots at which they could refresh themselves. The route was lined with the bones of slaves who had perished of thirst on the *coffles* which took them north, for this was the main slave route between the negroes of Bornu and the Arab traders of the north. Denham describes how, when he was dozing on his horse in the heat of the sun, "I was suddenly awakened by a cracking under my feet, which startled me excessively. I found that my steed had stepped upon a perfect skeleton of two human beings, cracking their brittle bones under his feet, and by one trip of his foot separating a skull from the trunk, which rolled like a ball before him. This event gave me a sensation which it took some time to remove."

On February 4, 1823, they made their first discovery when they saw Lake Chad at a place called Wauri on the north-western shore. The lake provided a marvellous contrast to the desert through which they had passed, its waters teeming with fish, its shores the home of herds of buffalo, antelope and elephant; there were even "good-looking negresses."

Ten days later they crossed the river Yobe (or Yeou), which ran into it from the west. Could this be the far-famed Niger? It hardly looked like it, being a shallow stream only fifty yards wide. "As I expected," wrote Denham, "every one of the Arabs said this was the Nile." Oudney thought there might be a "probability" that it was the Niger, on the strength of which Barrow trumpeted the news in the *Quarterly Review* that it "unquestionably is the Niger." On which a rival in *Blackwood's* laughed at the idea that "this petty stream was the GREAT RIVER NIGER." As the months passed, and as they got to know the Chad area better, even the explorers gave up the pretence that this was so.

They were welcomed at Kukuwa (or Kuka), the capital of Bornu, lying twelve miles west of the lake, by its remarkable ruler, Sheikh Mohammed El Kanemi, who had recently defeated Fulani invaders sent by Sultan Bello of Sokoto, another intelligent potentate whom Clapperton was to meet later. It was their first taste of the comparatively sophisticated way of life which prevailed in Central Africa, quite unknown to Europeans because it was hemmed in by deserts on all sides. Denham describes the scene:

"We were ushered into the presence of this Sheikh of Spears. We found him in a small dark room, sitting on a carpet, plainly dressed in a blue tobe [shirt] of Soudan and a shawl turban. Two negroes were on each side of him, armed with pistols, and on his carpet lay a brace of these instruments. Firearms were hanging in different parts of the room. . . . His personal appearance was prepossessing, apparently not more than forty-five or forty-six, with an expressive countenance and a benevolent smile. We delivered our letter from the Bashaw; and after he had read it, he inquired 'what was our object in coming?' We answered 'to see the country merely, and to give an account of its inhabitants, produce and appearance; as our sultan was desirous of knowing every part of the globe.' His reply was 'that we were welcome! and whatever he could show us would give him pleasure: that he had ordered huts to be built for us in the town; and that we might then go, accompanied by one of his people, to see them; and that when we were recovered from the fatigue of our long journey, he would be happy to see us.' With this we took our leave."

Later, they returned with their presents – a double-barrelled shotgun made by Wilkinson's, a pair of pistols, some red and blue cloth and a set of china. Next day a camel load of fresh fish was thrown on the ground before their hut, to be followed by another that evening. Honours were even when Clapperton fixed some Congreve rockets on three spears in front of the Sheikh's residence and fired them off amid the delighted shrieks of the populace. It was a later consignment of these rockets which cemented the friendship of the Sheikh and the Europeans.

The start to what might have been a fruitful period of exploration was auspicious, but the domestic tensions between the travellers now exploded in a shocking attack on Clapperton's character by Denham. He accused him of having had homosexual relations with an Arab during the journey across the desert. In those less permissive days it was a charge – or rather a slander, since it was never openly made – which would have resulted in a duel at home. Clapperton had previously resented the way in which Denham treated him as a common soldier and angry letters had been exchanged. Now Denham hinted maliciously at his private behaviour: "The continued extreme impropriety of your conduct is no less discreditable to the mission and the country than to your self as an officer." Asked what he referred to, he mentioned a rumour started by an aggrieved Arab several weeks back. "No one who knows Clapperton will ever listen to such a charge against him," the scandalised Oudney told Warrington. "He is not the man to disgrace himself so – the whole has so much improbability that the most disinterested would pronounce it a Vile, Malicious report."

But the damage was done, so that any concerted action on the part of the three men was now out of the question for the rest of the expedition. Denham went off on his own to join a big slave hunt, on which he nearly lost his life. His only reward was another reprimand from London for countenancing such "disgraceful proceedings." Naturally he says nothing about this in his narrative, nor does he mention Oudney and Clapperton's excursions to discover the river Shari running into the lake from the south. When he himself saw the river some months later, he pretended that it was his own discovery.

Again the question was raised, was the Shari the Niger? It was a mile wide, and as usual the natives called it the Nile. If it was not, "Where is the Niger? The Yeou is the only probably river coming from the Soudan, and it is too small almost. . . . The Shad has no outlet, so it wastes by evaporation all the waters of both the great Sharee and Yeou." Even that did not shake Barrow's conviction that "no doubt whatever can remain that the Yeou is the Niger." The last sentence of his review of Denham's book three years later runs: "The junction of the waters of this great lake with others of the Nile is not only *possible*, but extremely *probable*."

The biggest mistake made by the mission was to leave the

question thus open. Had Denham taken the trouble to travel right round the lake, instead of making futile excursions to the south of it, the Chad–Nile theory could no longer be entertained. Oudney guessed that the lake had no outlet, but Denham failed to prove it. The internal dissensions which ruined the expedition left the exploration of the area to Denham, while Oudney and Clapperton, who were no longer on speaking terms with him, struck out westward.

There was, however, one excursion from Kuka on which all three travelled together. This was to the province of Manga, lying some way up the Yobe river. On their return, the whole expedition nearly terminated in disaster. The rains had set it, so that water poured through the thatched roof of the hut which they so miserably shared. All four went down with fever. Clapperton became delirious; Hillman lay on the point of death: Oudney's consumptive cough left him sleepless every night; even the tough Major took to his bed. Fortunately, relations with the Sheikh and the townspeople remained friendly, so that with the onset of the dry season all, save Oudney, recovered; but it was agreed that thenceforward they should go their ways separately.

In December 1823 Oudney and Clapperton decided to go west to Kano. The former was still so weak that El Kanemi tried to dissuade him: "Surely your health is not such as to risk such a journey." "Why," replied the Doctor, "if I stay here, I shall die, and probably sooner, as travelling always improves my health." The Sheikh was right: Oudney died soon after they set out.

Their departure left Denham free to explore the Chad area on his own account. He was, indeed, accompanied on one of his excursions (they were nothing more) by Midshipman Toole, who arrived at top speed from Malta when Tyrwhitt was recalled. He was a cheerful young man who played the flute, but he died within a few weeks of his arrival at Logone on the west bank of the river Shari. In the following May Tyrwhitt returned to go with Denham on another excursion, but he too died of fever in the autumn.

Only Hillman was left, happily building a carriage for the Sheikh, when Clapperton returned from his western journey and Denham from his eastern one. The two men who most disliked each other were thus left alone for their return home, and since they had not been on speaking terms for some time, they had to make plans by writing notes to each other.

Clapperton's journey to Kano and Sokoto (Sackatoo, as he spelled it) had been the most fruitful part of the mission, just as his account of it is far more readable than Denham's prolix narrative. It is a good sea officer's journal, meticulous in its notes about the weather, the temperature etc., the country he passed through and the conversations he had with those he met. Left on his own, his stature as an explorer immediately increases, so that for the first time we see him as an enterprising as well as an attractive personality.

He and Oudney set out for the Hausa country at the end of the year with a *coffle* of a hundred men. Oudney's health deteriorated rapidly. The cold nights alternating with sweltering days made his cough much worse. He was soon asking his companion to entrust his papers to Barrow, though he continued to give medical advice to all who asked him. He died on January 12, 1824, on the road to Murmur, soon after writing his last despatch home informing the Colonial Secretary that he intended to reach Nupe "and see in that country the river or lake Quorra. I am a great invalid and hope the present journey will recruit me a little. I am perfectly convinced that the prospect of it is what alone has kept me up."

Clapperton, who himself suffered from malaria throughout the journey, recorded his friend's death with this comment: "To me, his friend and fellow traveller, labouring also under disease, and now left alone amid a strange people, and proceeding through a country which has hitherto never been trod by European foot, the loss was severe and afflicting in the extreme." He read the burial service over the grave, but soon afterwards Oudney's remains were disinterred and burned by the natives because they thought the doctor must have been a magician as well as an infidel.

Clapperton continued to Kano, the first of the big walled Hausa towns, the prosperity of which surprised him. It was a place of some 40,000 inhabitants, of whom over half were slaves and it was the situation of the most important market in Central Africa – Clapperton even bought a green umbrella made in Bond Street there. But it was built around a central morass, into the stagnant waters of which all the drains flowed. The Emir was hospitable, so that Clapperton stayed for some time hoping to recover from malaria. One of his entertainments was organising a boxing match between two professionals of a sport which certainly knew no Queensberry rules: when one of the contestants tried to strangle the other he had to stop the match.

The country through which he passed on the next stage of his lonely journey to Sokoto was fertile, wooded, well populated and altogether a welcome change after the deserts further north. As he approached the capital of the Fulani empire he spruced himself up as befitted the first representative of another race to visit those parts. He put on his blue naval frock coat, trimmed with gold lace and epaulettes, his white trousers and silk stockings, though on his head he continued to wear a turban. Thus arrayed, he entered one of the thirteen gates of the city on March 16 and the next day had the first of many enjoyable interviews with the Sultan.

Sultan Bello was the son of the great Fulani conqueror, Usuman dan Fodio, who in 1805 founded this new town as the centre of the Muslim faith, which it remains today in what we should call northern Nigeria. He was now forty-four years old, a tall, distinguished, heavily built man with a

curling beard and intelligent black eyes. Clapperton found
him astonishingly friendly and extremely well informed
about the outer world, which had never heard of him. When
Clapperton gave him his presents, the one which pleased
Bello the most was the pocket sextant, Clapperton tactfully
pointing out that it would always inform him of the correct
direction for his religious observances. "Every thing is
wonderful," exclaimed Bello, "but you are the greatest
curiosity of all! What can I give that is most acceptable to
the King of England?"

"Abandon the slave trade," Clapperton boldly suggested.

"What, have you no slaves in England?"

"No. Whenever a slave sets foot in England, he is from
that moment free."

"What do you do, then, for servants?"

"We hire them for a stated period, and give them regular
wages; nor is any person in England permitted to strike
another; and the very soldiers are fed, clothed and paid by
the government."

"God is Great! You are a beautiful people."

During the three months Clapperton spent at Sokoto he
had many such conversations. From one of the old men at
Bello's court he heard details about the death of Mungo Park
which confirmed Isaaco's account. He was also told that
some of Park's books were in the possession of the Sultan of
Yauri. Bello himself knew all about it, as well as about Lord
Exmouth's bombardment of Algiers and the British dominion
in India, something which may well have made him hesitate
about becoming too friendly with this representative of the
British Empire. It has even been suggested that it was a
warning on this score which he gave to the governor of
Timbuktu which hastened Laing's death and that he may
purposely have misled Clapperton about the course of the
lower Niger. On the other hand, he often asked him to
persuade the British government to open trade relations and

even wrote a request to this effect to George IV. In all his conversations with Clapperton he unaffectedly praised the British people. "Having heard of our newspapers, he desired me to send for them, calling them the News of the World. Being set to read extracts from them, I happened to mention that thousands of them were printed daily, when he exclaimed 'God is Great: You are a wonderful people!' "

It was not long before Clapperton got round to the real object of his visit, the course of the Niger. Bello replied to his enquiries, though in fact he seems to have been ignorant of any geography outside his dominions. On the sand he drew a map (later copied by one of his scribes) to show the course of the Quorra from Timbuktu to Bussa, where he noted that Park's boat was lost, and on into the Nupe country, where it turned sharply east, though he asserted that it entered the sea at a place called Fundah. This, however, was contradicted by the superscription on the map: "This is the sea (river) of Kowarra (Quorra) which reaches Egypt, and which is called the Nile." No wonder that Barrow was pleased at the story Clapperton brought back, though by this time the latter was convinced that the course of the river lay due south into the Bight of Benin. A possible explanation of Bello's error is that, knowing nothing about the lower Niger, he mistook its tributary, the Benue, for that river, because the latter joins the Niger at a point about thirty miles south of Fundah, now identified as Panda. But there remains the possibility of a deliberate error in order to mislead the Christian traveller.

Clapperton would have followed his hunch southward had not Bello dissuaded him from entering a country which he said was the seat of war at the moment. Clapperton was also a very sick man, so he regretfully decided to return the way he had come. When he took his leave, Bello gave him a letter to George IV requesting that a trade mission should be sent. He gave Clapperton his blessing, "and praying for my safe arrival in England, and speedy return to Sackatoo, he affectionately bade me farewell."

He returned to Kuka on July 8, where Denham joined him two days later. There was the usual difference of opinion about the route home, Denham making a wild suggestion that they should go via Egypt. In the end they reached Warrington's house at Tripoli, where he had another row with the consul, so that only Clapperton thanked him for the support he had given to the mission over the past two years. At the same time Clapperton demanded an enquiry into the scandalous charge that had been brought against him, but Warrington persuaded him to let the matter drop. In June, 1825, the two travellers were back in England.

The positive results of the Mission to Bornu were twofold. In the first place, as Barrow pointed out in his review of Denham's book, "we now know where the great kingdoms of Mandara, Bornou and Houssa are to be placed on the map: in what latitude and longitude are situated the various cities and towns, whose names only we have heard, and one of which, Bornou, had been guessed out of its place more than six hundred miles." A new and comparatively civilised part of the world, hitherto totally unknown, had been revealed, in which a skilful, prosperous and well-disposed black population existed.

As to the Niger, Barrow continued, "The information obtained by Clapperton has entangled the question more than before," – by which he meant the conflict between his own hypothesis, Bello's map and Clapperton's conviction that the answer lay in the Bight of Benin. Both Warrington and Clapperton passed on Bello's information to Gordon Laing, but, as we have seen, that conceited young man was only interested in reaching the Niger before Clapperton, so he showed no gratitude.

Hugh Clapperton was off again only three months after his

return. He left his papers with Barrow, who insisted on adding the journal of his visit to Sokoto to Denham's narrative. The latter remained at home to reap the credit for whatever success the mission had achieved and he was rewarded by being appointed governor of Sierra Leone. He died there in 1828, soon after taking over his duties. One can only agree with the verdict of the editor of his journal that "it remains difficult to recall in the chequered history of geographical discovery – a vocation that has attracted many very odd characters – a more odious man than Dixon Denham."

Clapperton's anxiety to be off again so soon was due partly to the fear that Laing might forestall him and partly due to the fact that the best time to reach Sokoto from the south was during the dry season. The Colonial Office agreed, even though it was obvious that he was still a sick man. He was given his instructions to establish relations with Sultan Bello, as that potentate had desired, and to deliver a reply to his letter, the chief contents of which was a reiterated request that he should give up the slave trade. As an object which was clearly of secondary importance to the authorities, Clapperton was told that it was highly desirable to trace the course of the river which passed through Timbuktu, "which has been known in modern times by the name of the Niger." The insertion of the anti-slavery clause in Clapperton's instructions makes this expedition a turning point in West African exploration, because henceforth this was to be the principal official objective, geographical discovery now assuming a secondary role.

Clapperton sailed from Portsmouth on August 27, 1825, in the sloop *Brazen*, which was destined for the anti-slavery patrol off the West Coast of Africa. With him there was a friend called Dr Dickson, who was to have taken up residence as consul at Sokoto but decided to go to Dahomey instead and was never heard of again. There was also Captain

Pearce RN and a naval surgeon called Dr Morrison, both of whom died soon after reaching Africa. As interpreter in the Hausa country, he took with him an old liberated slave called Pasko or Pascoe, whose real name was Abu Becr, a confirmed thief and womaniser in spite of his remarkably ugly face, but an amusing rascal when sober. And there was also Richard Lemon Lander, Clapperton's personal servant, aged twenty-one.

In Lander we meet the most attractive of all African explorers. His journals are more readable than any others, though the credit for this must go to his younger brother John, because the few scraps of Richard's own writings which have survived among the Colonial Office papers show him to have been totally ignorant of orthography. As he was of humble birth and received hardly any education, this is not surprising. John, on the other hand, belonged to the Age of Sensibility, echoes of which in some high-flown passages spoil the simplicity of Richard's character as displayed in his extraordinary adventures. Moreover, for official correspondence we know that Richard employed an amanuensis, merely signing his name in a laborious hand at the bottom of the page.

Richard Lander was obsessed by a love of travel. Born at Truro in 1804 the son of an innkeeper, he left home at the age of nine because of "a series of domestic misfortunes unpleasant to particularise." Starting as a houseboy, he became the servant of a number of gentlemen in various parts of the world before he volunteered to act as such to Clapperton when still only twenty-one years old. His only qualifications as an explorer in his own right were the two basic ones – love of travel ("the very sound of Africa always made my heart flutter") and a sturdy frame which a friend of his called as broad as it was long. To this must be added an amazing resilience of spirits, so that however cast down he might be by loneliness or fever he was soon cheerful again, blowing tunes on the bugle which he took with him on his travels and getting on well with almost everyone he met. In sum, he was a sturdy, simple, friendly young man, with deep religious convictions.

In Clapperton he found the perfect master, or rather companion, because on the march all social distinctions were cast aside, so that the two men shared their hardships on a footing of perfect equality which soon ripened into deep friendship. It was a just reward for Lander's devotion that, after bringing home Clapperton's papers, he himself went out again with his brother to complete the discovery of the long-sought Niger.

For Clapperton's last journey there are thus two sources: his own journal, edited by John Barrow, and Lander's account, which is much more complete and vivid. Clapperton's often illegible notes, written in pencil in a tiny notebook which has been preserved at the Public Record Office, explain Barrow's complaint that they were written "in the most loose and careless manner. . . . Clapperton was evidently a man of no education; he nowhere disturbs the progress of the day's narrative by any reflections of his own." No wonder, seeing that he was seriously ill most of the time. The miracle was that he got so far before dying of malaria and dysentery. After editing his journal, Barrow admitted that the course of the Niger seemed to be southerly. At the same time he insisted that it should no longer be called the Niger, as Park knew it, but the Quorra, the termination of which "is still open to conjecture." It was Lander, whom he called at first in a patronising way "an interesting young man", but whom he later came to admire and support, who finally destroyed his hypothesis.

Lander's own account was written to supplement that of "my lamented master." It is obviously compiled by his brother from memories dictated by Richard, because the only surviving pieces in his own hand are quite ungrammatical. It contains a much livelier description of the countries through which they passed, interspersed with general reflections. It was he alone of the explorers who was impressed by the carvings of the Yoruba people. It is he who castigates the slave trade, though, from his own experience in the West Indies he puts slavery into its proper proportions:

"The slave in most interior districts is treated with infinitely greater lenity and kindness than among the less civilised natives of the sea coast; and the condition of the slaves of European planters is not to be compared, for happiness and comfort. . . . Upon the whole, I should consider the situation of domestic slaves in Africa to be more enviable than that of the household servant in Europe."

With his experience, he should know. Finally, it is Lander who makes the interesting comparison between Fulani Islamic imperialism with that of Russia, both "making rapid and gigantic strides towards enormous despotism."

After the usual anti-slave trade cruise, during which they intercepted two slavers and visited the *barracoons* on shore, where slaves were housed awaiting shipment, HMS *Brazen* anchored at Badagry near Lagos on November 29. There was no sign of the messengers Bello had promised to send, nor had anyone heard of Fundah where he had said that the Niger terminated. The fact was that the belt of tropical rain forest virtually cut off any communication or knowledge between north and south.

There were affecting scenes when the explorers left the ship for a journey from which none expected to return, such was the reputation of the country. Lander covered the general embarrassment by playing "Over the hills and far away" on what he called his bugle horn, an instrument which greatly impressed the natives on later stages of the expedition.

After a heavy drinking party with the caboceer or chief of Badagry, who was presented with the inevitable umbrella, the party and their considerable baggage train marched inland by narrow forest paths. Clapperton was soon suffering again from bouts of fever, so that he had to be carried in a hammock much of the way; nor could they sleep at night on account of the noise which remains a feature of African village life: "It is beyond the power of even African despotism to silence a woman's tongue; in sickness and in health, and at every stage, we have been obliged to endure their eternal loquacity and noise."

Having passed through the humid belt of forest and crossed the romantic mountains of Kong, they entered the more temperate and heavily populated country of the northern Yorubas. They were escorted into the capital, Katunga (Old Oyo), by soldiers and musicians to meet the king surrounded by four hundred of his wives. "A mild and kind people," Clapperton calls them, easily impressed when he fired off the Congreve rockets. Nevertheless, "the commerce of this country is almost entirely confined to slaves."

They stayed there seven weeks before moving on to Bussa on the Niger itself. There they found the people unwilling to talk about Park's death, the explanation given them being that he was mistaken for the advance guard of a Fulani invasion. Clapperton strangely describes Bussa as an island, whereas it is a town on the west bank: perhaps the river was then in flood. The crossing of the river remains almost unnoticed in his record; possibly he was too ill to feel any excitement about it. Among his rough notes it is evident at this stage that it was his own death, not Park's, which was uppermost in his mind, thus giving them a note of desperation: "I am so near crossing [the Niger?] that I am like a gamester desperate I would stake all." Even Lander does no more than note that its course was from NNE to SSE.

Close by, at a place called Wawaw or Wowow, they had the most amusing experience of their travels. They were lodged in the house of a rich widow called Zuma, of Arab

Crossing the Niger at Say: from H. Barth *Travels in North Africa* 1857

View of the Bahr Mandia oasis: a sketch by Hugh Clapperton in *Travels in Northern Africa* 1828

Captain Hugh Clapperton: from an engraving by Lupton after a portrait by Gildon Manton

descent and the owner, so she said, of a thousand slaves. She was monstrously ugly, a hill of flesh which accorded well with Arab ideas of beauty, but "a walking water butt" to the Europeans. Her eyes were painted with indigo, her hands and feet with henna, her "tremendous breasts" shaking as she moved. This formidable female, says Lander, "took it into her head to fall desperately in love with me, whose complexion, she affirmed, rivalled her own in whiteness." The young man was terribly embarrassed, especially as Clapperton treated the whole thing as a joke and egged on both parties. "For an hour together the widow would gaze intently on me, while the most amorous glances shot from her large, full and certainly beautiful eyes, which confused and disconcerted me not a little. . . . I was positively afraid, from the warmth and energy of Zuma's embraces, I should actually be pressed to death between her monstrous arms."

Eliciting no response from the servant, she turned her attentions to the master and when Clapperton rode out of town she followed him on horseback, wearing a cloak of gold silk and red morocco boots. "I thought this was carrying the joke a little too far," writes Clapperton after she tried to delay him, "and began to look very serious, on which she sent for a looking-glass, and looking at herself, then offering it to me, said, to be sure she was rather older than me, but very little, and what of that? This was too much, and I made my retreat as soon as I could, determined never to come to such close quarters with her again."

The Nupe (or Nyffe) country across the Niger was the scene of war, so that the way was dangerous as well as difficult for a man as sick as Clapperton now was. He was often carried in a hammock and had to cross the fords on Lander's shoulders. On July 20, 1826, they reached the city of Kano, about which Lander was no more favourably impressed than Clapperton had been on his previous visit. The central morass, into which dead slaves were thrown as if they were dogs, smelled worse than ever and the clouds of flies and mosquitoes which it bred certainly explains their ill health continuing. Pasko was always absconding, being brought back in irons and then escaping again to buy the favours of some woman with goods stolen from his masters. The rough entries in Clapperton's notebook made during their five weeks stay at this unhealthy spot tell their own story:

Monday	*25 – Waited on Sultan – had to wait a long time – ill with ague.*
Tuesday	*26 – ill all day.*
Wednesday	*27 – ill.*
Thursday	*28 – ill all day a ? Courier*
Friday	*29 – a little better.*
Saturday	*30 – Verey hill, unable to [eat] anything in* Lander's hand.
Sunday	*31 – No better, a day of rain.*
Monday	*1 August – a little better. . . .*

The rest of the pocket book consists of scribbles on the state of the weather written in pencil because pen and ink were finished.

Communications between Sultan Bello's dominions in the west and Bornu in the east were now severed by war. Bello himself was busy in the field with his army, so that Clapperton's reception at Kano was far less hospitable than it had been on his first visit. Leaving Lander there confined to his bed with fever, Clapperton pressed on by himself to Sokoto in order to obtain a personal interview with Bello. On arrival he was told that he would be lodged in his old house, but before he could reach his quarters he received a command to visit the Sultan, "who would excuse every thing about my dress, as he was anxious to see me. I accordingly dismounted and was instantly shown into the residence of Bello, which was formed of a number of huts, screened off by cloth fixed to poles, making quite a little village of itself. His reception of me was most kind and gratifying; he asked after the health of the king of England, and if we were still at peace, and how I had found all my friends. He was surprised when I said I had not seen them, and that I had remained only four months in England. He said he had not received my letters. He asked me if I had not experienced a great many difficulties in getting through Youriba; said he had heard of me when I was at Katunga, and that he had sent a messenger to that place to assist me in getting through; and had also sent another to Koolfu; but neither of whom, as I told him, had I seen."

The welcome, however, belied Bello's mistrust of his visitor's intentions, notably after he heard that Clapperton was carrying presents to Bornu, with which state he was now at war. Nor do Clapperton's presents to this prince of the Islamic faith seem quite appropriate: the New Testament in Arabic, the Psalms of David, a History of the Tartars and Euclid's Elements.

Relations between the two men worsened as Clapperton fell ill again and Bello found himself more closely involved in military operations, on some of which Clapperton accompanied him. There was no longer the warmth of their previous meetings. He was suspected as a spy and his presents for Bornu were at length confiscated, despite Clapperton's protests that such a search of his hut and the theft of his belongings only befitted "a nation of robbers." In the end, Clapperton vowed that he never wanted to see the Sultan again.

Meanwhile Lander lay sick at Kano until, in December, letters arrived summoning him to Sokoto. Though he was himself very ill, "I was determined to see my master before I died." He reached the capital on December 23. On Christmas Day, writes Clapperton, "I gave my servant Richard one sovereign out of six I have left, as a Christmas gift; for he is well deserving and has never once shown a want of courage or enterprise unworthy of an Englishman."

For a few weeks after their reunion the two men enjoyed tolerably good health, though Clapperton's spirits continued to be depressed after what he called Bello's duplicity: "he spoke with warmth of the artful and unhandsome conduct of the Sultan and to the hour of his death I never observed him to smile."

Occasionally they were able to escape the confines of the yard surrounding their hut in order to go shooting, and in the evenings they talked over their cigars (their only remaining luxury, now that stocks of tea were exhausted), read the Bible to each other, or sang the songs of their homeland. Lander often played a tune on his bugle horn: "How often have the pleasing strains of 'Sweet, sweet Home' resounded through the melancholy streets of Soccatoo!" Clapperton, with his gaunt face, feverish eyes and a beard flowing to his waist (the envy of every Arab), had a patriarchal if ghastly appearance. Both wore white turbans, a flowing *tobe* or shirt, and a broad belt with pistols and daggers stuck in it, so that Lander often told his master that he looked more like a mountain chieftain than a naval officer. No plans for escaping from Sokoto were possible as long as the war with Bornu continued and Clapperton's ill health made him weaker every day.

On March 12 he suffered another severe attack of dysentery. The last entry in his journal is dated the previous night. For a month his condition deteriorated, and although Lander himself was suffering from fever, he had to attend his master every minute of the day and night, feeding him, fanning him for hours on end, washing him or carrying him in his arms out to the shade of the only tree in the yard in order to escape the stifling heat of their bee-hive hut, heat which now reached 109° Fahrenheit in the afternoons.

After twenty days illness Clapperton was reduced to a skeleton; "there could not be a more pitiable object in the universe than was my poor dear master." Too weak to write himself, he gave Lander his dying instructions which are contained in a letter written by Lander, which has no punctuation whatever in the original:

"What my master said to me at Sakatoo, April, 1827. Richard, i am going to die. I cannot help shedding tears, has he had behaved like a father to me since i had been with him. We went into the hut. He whas then laying in a shade outside. He said, Richard, come here my dear boy, its the will of God, it cant be helped. Bear yourself up under all troubles like a man and an english man, do not be affraid and no one will hurt you. I do not fear that, sir, its for the loss of you who has been a father to me since when i have ben with you. My dear boy i will tell you what to do. Take great care of my journals and when you arrive in London go to my agents and tell them to send directly for my uncul and tell him it was my wish that he would go with me to the colonoal office and delever the journals, that they might not say their were anything missing. My little money, my close and evrything i have belongs to you. Bello will lend you money to buy cammels and provisions and send you home over the desert with the gaffle, and when you arrive at Tripoli Mr Warrington will give you what money you want and send you home the first opportunity. . . . Writ down the names of the towns you go throw and all purticulars. And if you get safe home with the journals i have no doubt of your being well rewarded for your truble."

As will be seen, Lander found it impossible to return by the proposed route and chose the opposite direction; nor was he ever rewarded for his pains.

On April 13, 1827, Hugh Clapperton died at Sokoto at the age of forty. Richard buried him at a spot five miles outside the town. "The corpse was borne on a camel to the brink of the pit, and I planted the flag close to it; then, uncovering my head, and opening a prayer book, I read the impressive service of the Church of England over the remains of my valued master – the English flag waving slowly and mournfully over them at the same moment. Not a single soul listened to this peculiarly distressing ceremony, for the slaves were quarrelling with each other the whole time it lasted."

6

The Solution of the Mystery:
The Landers

For a fortnight after the death of his master, Richard Lander lay desperately ill in his hut at Sokoto. Unable to rise from his mat, sweating and shivering by turns from fever in the stifling heat, he was tended by Pasko alone. The strain of the previous months spent nursing Clapperton day and night obviously caused this relapse, and there was now the deep fear that his own end was near.

It is hard to imagine a more severe test of the fortitude of the "little Christian," as the Africans called him on account of his diminutive stature, than the situation in which he found himself. Just over twenty years old, he lay abandoned in the heart of darkness, without health, money or companionship. The Arabs in the town were now his open enemies. With no knowledge of the geography of the country or its language, he had neither the strength nor the means to make plans for the long journey home. At times he gave himself up for lost. His hut was searched for arms and it was made plain that his presence in the town was unwelcome because he was the servant of a spy and an infidel. No wonder that Sokoto was the one town in Africa that he came to hate. He must get away before he died there, so by judicious bribery he persuaded a courtier to ask the Sultan to get him out of the place.

Bello summoned him to his presence to ask him by what route he proposed to return. That suggested by Clapperton did not appeal to Lander, who distrusted the "wily and

treacherous" type of Arab who would be his companions on
the road north. He must have recalled the fate of other white
travellers in such company on the desert caravans, though he
could have yet heard of the murder of Gordon Laing on
such a *coffle* near Timbuktu. He therefore told Bello that he
wished to go south by the way he had come. Bello said that
was impossible because of the rainy season: he must go to
Kano, where an official would provide him with the means
to go north. Having no money, Lander obeyed.

On May 3, 1827, he and Pasko joined a huge caravan of
some four thousand persons going to that place, many of
them fanatical pilgrims on their way to Mecca. Short as the
journey was, it was a terrible experience for a man in
Lander's state of health. At one point he fell exhausted to
the ground. As he lay there, other travellers spurned him as
a Christian dog. Pasko disappeared to eat his master's
provisions, so that he might well have perished amid cries of
"He is a Kafir; let him die!" had not a young Fulani taken
pity on him.

"Christian, Christian, why don't you go on?"

"I am faint for want of water; no one will relieve me; how
can I go on?"

The man gave him a small calabash of water, part of
which was used to bathe the mouth and nostrils of Lander's
equally exhausted horse. When others upraided the man for
helping a Christian, he showed them a gun, saying that he
had got it from Christians and they were good men.

At Kano Lander was given enough money to purchase
provisions but not enough to enable him to join the caravan
going north. He was not sorry to be thus compelled to go
south, for in that direction two routes presented themselves.
One was his former way through Nupe, the other led to
Fundah, which he and Clapperton must often have discussed
as the supposed termination of the Niger. His master had
warned him to avoid the unsettled conditions on the former

route, so, "feeling an earnest desire, which I could not repress, to visit Fundah, on the banks of the Niger, and trace that much-talked-of river in a canoe to Benin," his curiosity led him to choose the latter. A pathetic letter which he sent to Warrington from Kano in May, telling him about Clapperton's death, is a good example of the way he wrote:

"That which i expect in 10 days is proceed to the sea side the way we came, or a nearer way 10 days due south of Culfo to Fundah which i expect is the Bite of Benin. Here the carra [Quorra] runs to it. This river is called the Niger, and the sultan of Calfo asshures me of the road being safe. I will go, has it will be a great advantage to the English. I send a copy of this journal from Katunga to this town by an arab to whom on delivery them you will give him 50 dollars. I remain your most Obedient Humble Servant, Richard Lemon Lander, Servant to the late Capt. Clapperton."

He never reached Fundah, because conditions proved impossible and he was warned that he would be put to death if the inhabitants of those parts knew that he came from the north. He therefore recrossed the Niger to make his way to Wowow, where he knew that the king was friendly and that he would be able to regain his previous route. Some idea of the straits he was in when suffering from dysentery as well as fever is his comment on the food available – a little boiled Indian corn, "for I by no means relished the huge luncheons of roasted dogs which were served twice a day."

Across the Niger in the Yoruba country the people were more friendly; the mode of expression is his brother's:

"I take this opportunity of expressing my high admiration of the amiable conduct of the African females towards me; in sickness and in health; in prosperity and in adversity – their kindness and affection were ever the same. They have danced and sung with me in health, grieved with me in sorrow, and shed tears of compassion at the recital of my misfortunes. Through whatever region I have wandered, whether slave or free, I have invariably found a chord of tenderness and trembling pity to vibrate in the heart of African women; and I never in my life knew one of them to bestow on me a single unpleasant look or angry word."

At Wowow he was received with courtesy for the first time for many months. The king set him to work cleaning some muskets which had evidently belonged to Park's party because on them he found the marks of the Tower armoury. His own firearms were taken from him, but in recompense he was given a beautiful little mare. Moreover, he was "serenaded with the wild music of a guitar, accompanied by a female voice" – an emissary from the lovelorn widow Zuma, now confined to her house because she was suspected of seditious intentions.

When he was permitted to continue his journey to Katunga, conditions became even better. "At this time I lived like an eastern prince, generally subsisting on the best the country afforded; and towards evening, when I felt fatigued, Aboudah [a female slave given him by the king of Zeg Zeg] used to bathe my temples with the juice of limes, and after washing my feet, either sing or fan me to sleep." He even organised his little party – Pasko and his wife, Aboudah and Joudie, his domestic slaves – in the accepted manner of nineteenth century travellers. Every evening after the tents were pitched, "it was my usual custom to read aloud, from a book of Common Prayer, some portion of its contents, making the servants sit around me in a circle." One cannot imagine what his black audience made of this performance. One only trusts that they were impressed by his simple piety.

The king of Katunga did his best to persuade him to stay there for the rest of his life by promising to make him prime minister, generalissimo, whatever he wanted – even four of his daughters for wives. Lander was tempted: "An Englishman, tired of his country, would be delighted with Yariba, for it is a fine kingdom, people with a mild, affectionate and unassuming race, by whom he would be regarded almost as a deity, and amongst whom he would end his days with pleasure." It was the sort of pipe dream familiar to beach-combers on a South Sea island, though Dr Baikie was to find that it was almost true. To a man of Lander's humble station in life it must have had a strong appeal; what repelled him was the food – dogs, cats, a dozen stewed rats for dinner, fried locusts and caterpillars, which Pasko esteemed a delicacy.

After a happy stay of many months he left for the coast in high spirits. But when on November 21 he reached Badagry after an absence of two years, during which he had completed a journey which must be regarded as the most extraordinary ever made by a man so young and inexperienced, he was once more plunged into despair. The Portuguese slave traders, led by the Da Souza family, detested him as the representative of a country which was trying to destroy their livelihood. The depraved caboceer and his court, who battened on the trade, made the town, as Lander called it, a city of blood, populated by "without comparison the most rude and barbarous people of the whole continent of Africa." Just outside his hut he witnessed the murder of two women by emissaries of the caboceer, who, having cut their throats, hung their limbs on a fetish tree. Hundreds of unsold slaves were often drowned in the river merely in order to clear stock. Human sacrifice was common, while in the forest he found a fetish tree which so revolted him that he fainted at the sight:

"The huge branches of the fetish tree, groaning beneath their burden of human flesh and bones, and sluggishly waving in consequence of the hasty retreat of the birds of prey; the intense and almost insufferable heat of a vertical sun; the intolerable odour of the corrupt corpses; the heaps of human heads, many of them apparently staring at me from hollows which had once sparkled with living eyes; the

awful stillness of the place, disturbed only by the frightful
screaming of voracious vultures, as they flapped their sable
wings almost in my face – all tended to overpower me."

This was the sort of place where he had to wait for weeks
for a ship to take him to the nearest British outpost. As the
days passed, the Portuguese persuaded the caboceer that he
was a dangerous man who should be put to the poison test.
He was arrested and dragged before a council of witch
doctors, who presented him with a bowl of clear-looking
liquid and informed him that it would only kill him if he
was a bad man.

"I took the bowl in my trembling hands and gazed for a
moment at the sable countenances of my judges; but not a
single look of compassion shone upon any of them; a dead
silence prevailed in the gloomy sanctuary of skulls; every eye
was intently fixed upon me; and seeing no possibility of
escape, I offered up internally a short prayer to the Throne
of Mercy – the God of Christians – and hastily swallowed
the fetish, dashing the poison chalice to the ground. A low
murmur ran through the assembly; they all thought I should
instantly have expired, or at least have discovered symptoms
of severe agony, but detecting no such tokens, they arose
simultaneously and made way for me to leave the hut. On
getting into the open air, I found my poor slaves in tears;
they had come, they said, to catch a last glimpse of their
master; but when they saw me alive and at liberty, they
leaped and danced with joy, and prepared a path for me
through the dense mass of armed people. These set up an
astounding shout at my unexpected appearance, and seemed
greatly pleased that I had not fallen a victim to the influence
of the fearful fetish. On arriving at my dwelling, I took
instant and powerful means to eject the venonomous poison
from my stomach, and happily succeeded in the attempt."

Even though his survival earned him some popularity in
the town, he was warned not to go out unarmed for fear the

Portuguese traders might assassinate him. After several weeks of anxiety there arrived a message from a ship in the bay, accompanied by a bottle of gin. It was addressed to "The White Traveller on Shore at Badagry" and signed by Captain Laing of the brig *Maria*, London.

"Having been informed that a white man, a traveller in this country, was on shore here, I beg leave to acquaint you that I have come for the express purpose of conveying you to Cape Coast, and having come much out of my track, I beg you will repair on board with as little delay as possible."

The original text of the message, like so much else of Richard's original memoirs (the manuscript of which has disappeared), is paraphrased in the printed narrative, with the addition that the captain supposed that the traveller might have had some connection with the Clapperton mission.

Lander and his four slaves lost no time in getting down to the beach to meet the ship's boat. As they approached the brig, the yards were manned to welcome the young adventurer on board. He was taken to Cape Coast Castle, where he was given a passage home in HMS *Esk*, since he enjoyed official status as an employee of the Colonial Office; but as the ship had to complete her anti-slavery patrol before going home, it meant that he was taken to Fernando Po (where he met Dixon Denham, though no details are given of his conversation with Clapperton's old enemy), St Helena and Ascension before reaching Portsmouth on April 30, 1828.

In London he faithfully handed over Clapperton's papers, which, as we have seen, were passed on to Barrow, but no reward for his services was given to him. He revisited Truro after an absence of thirteen years, where he appears to have got married. There he obtained a job in the excise office, but we soon find him writing to Whitehall, complaining that recurrent fits of fever made it impossible for him to continue in an outside job. He asks for a clerkship and when this too failed he got a job as a porter at the Customs House. It is not surprising that as soon as another Niger expedition was proposed he volunteered with alacrity.

"Would not Lander, who has been pressing to go again, be the fittest person to send?" Barrow asked the Colonial Under-Secretary in September, 1829, when the expedition was first proposed. "No one in my opinion would make their way so well, and with a bundle of beads and other trinkets, we could land him somewhere about Bonny and let him find his way."

Richard accepted this casual mission, provided that his younger brother John was allowed to accompany him. Since John asked for no salary (nor did he ever receive any reward), this was agreed by a department of state which treated the whole expedition in as miserly a fashion as it had done with earlier explorers. Richard was offered £100 on his return, £100 for his wife, 300 dollars for the purchase of trade goods, and a free medicine chest. The contents of this chest are listed in the appendix to his narrative. Since it is the only record we possess of the sort of drugs then regarded as suitable for tropical explorers, it is a pitiable list:

> *4 bottles of calomel – purgative*
> *10 bottles of Epsom salts – purgative*
> *12 doz. Seidlitz powders – purgative*
> *1 oz. tartar emetic*
> *4 oz. ipececuanha – emetic*
> *2 lb. citric acid – in lieu of lemon juice – anti-scorbutic*
> *2 bottles carbonate of soda – for dysentery*
> *8 oz. blue pills – laxative*
> *2 pints opium – anodyne*
> *6 packets Dr James's powder – for perspiration*

Such, together with sponges, bandages, lancets, a pestle

and mortar to make their own pills, and useless items such as ginger, camphor and peppermint, is the typical eighteenth century pharmacopeia for the most dangerous climate in the world. The only mention of a new drug – quinine – is 4 oz sulphate of quinine "as a strengthener after fever": there is no record that the Landers ever used it, since they preferred calomel.

Their official instructions were to land at Badagry and go north to Katunga, from which they were to trace the course of the Quorra to its supposed termination at Fundah.

"If you should find that at Fundah the Quorra continues to flow to the southward, you are to follow it to the sea; but if it should be found to turn off to the eastward, in which case it will probably fall into Lake Tshad, you are to follow its course in that direction, as far as you can venture to do, with due regard to your personal safety, even to Bornou; in which case it will be for you to determine whether it may not be advisable to return home by way of Fezzan and Tripoli. . . . In short, having once gained the banks of the Quorra, you are to follow its course, if possible, to its termination, wherever that may be."

The two young Cornishmen left Portsmouth on January 9, 1830, for Cape Coast Castle, where they picked up old Pasko, who welcomed them with a huge grin on his ape-like face. At Accra, by Barrow's influence, they transferred to HM brig *Clinker* under the command of Lieutenant H. J. Matson, one of the most successful officers on the anti-slave trade patrol, who had already liberated over a thousand slaves. He landed them at Badagry near by.

Their reception at that poisonous place was even cooler than before. Fortunately, the king was too busy preparing for a sacrifice of three hundred slaves to bother about the travellers. Having mulcted them of a quantity of gold dust, they were allowed to go on their way. They struck up country in the fantastic clothes which amused all the naked

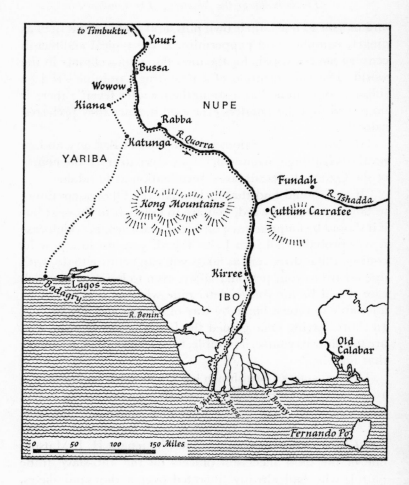

Africans who saw them – straw hats wider than umbrellas, scarlet tunics, full Turkish trousers. Richard always liked negroes, but John was at first repelled by them: "By and bye, doubtless, familiarity with black faces will reconcile me to them; but at present I am compelled to own that I cannot help feeling a very considerable share of aversion towards their jetty complexions."

Richard Lander by W. Brockedon

A Lancer of the Sultan of Begharmi: from Denham,
Clapperton and Oudney *Travels in Northern Africa* 1828

On horseback, accompanied by a score of porters who had to be changed at short intervals on the march, they passed through the country where the modern Ibadan lies and beyond the modern Oyo to Old Oyo or Katunga, the city of Old Oyo having been destroyed by Fulani invaders in 1837. The rains had broken, so that Richard was down with fever within a few weeks, but when they reached the more temperate uplands their spirits rose and the sound of his bugle horn was once more heard in the land. At Katunga they met old friends, with King Mansolah still pleased to see them. The town was obviously decaying, but there was peace and friendship to be found: "Instead of the jarring voices of women's tongues, which had annoyed and followed us at every stage of our journey from Badagry, we at length enjoy as much of composure and tranquillity as we can well desire."

After a rest of several weeks they made for Bussa, where they again enquired about Mungo Park's papers, but found nothing but an old nautical almanac which was to be purchased twenty-seven years later by Lieutenant Glover and presented to the Royal Geographical Society. To Richard's astonishment and embarrassment, he found the widow Zuma there. She had fled from Wowow, she exclaimed with much good humour, and had fallen on hard times, but she was stouter than ever, so that she could hardly squeeze through the door of their hut.

From Bussa they continued up the Niger, sometimes by boat, sometimes on horseback, as far as the big city of Yauri. They had no liking for the canoes on this part of the river because, as Park had found further north, they were constructed out of two half-trunks of trees sewn together and caulked with straw, so that they always leaked. They were to find that it was only on the lower Niger that the people were at home on the river, their canoes being made of single hollowed-out tree trunks. Yet on this middle part of the

river the banks were thickly populated and lined with
magnificent timber.

At Yauri they could find no help for their projected
voyage downstream, so they returned to Bussa for a canoe.
As usual, there were endless procrastinations and broken
promises before they determined to set out, come what may,
because their supply of trade goods was running out. They
had been told to follow the Niger to its mouth, but on
enquiry they were no wiser where this might be, so little did
the northern Yorubas know of the delta:

"Theories respecting the Niger are even more various and
contrary in this country than the hypotheses of the learned
in Europe on the subject. Scarcely two people are to be
found that agree in the same opinion, and their suppositions
are not confined to the course and termination, but include
the source of this mysterious river; yet, with all their talk, it
is easy to perceive that the natives are entirely ignorant of
the matter."

In the end they got their canoe, though they were warned
of robbers and every conceivable hazard lower down the
river. "Englishmen are gods of the water," Pasko stoutly
replied, having once crossed the ocean with them, "no evil
can befall them in boats, even though all Africa, or the whole
world, should fight against them." The witch doctors were
properly impressed. Permission was granted, so that after
wasting more time in the holiday festivities then being held
in the town, they embarked on September 20.

Their progress downstream was not as rapid as Park's,
because the two brothers and Pasko could not navigate the
large canoes by themselves. Crews had to be hired and
discharged every few miles until they reached Rabba in the
country of Nupe, where the king's admiral, the King of the
Dark Waters, provided them with a guide and a large flat-
bottomed boat built like a punt from a single piece of
timber, 15' long and 4' broad. Royal canoes were even

larger and the stream was filled with craft typical of a truly riverine society, whose members tended their boats as carefully as Arabs did their horses. Lander's account of such craft makes the Niger sound like the Ganges rather than the rapid rock-strewn stream which Park had known:

"So early as five o'clock in the morning our canoes were loaded and having breakfasted on a slice of yam, we were fully prepared to quit the island. But it was not deemed politic or proper to go away until the arrival of the great King of the Dark Waters, who was hourly expected, and who might be inclined to construe our departure into contempt, we consented to await his coming. Though we have been exposed to a thousand inconveniences and all manner of nuisances, yet rather than remain in a close black hut, full of men whose garments are generally covered with vermin; rather than do this, we stepped into our canoes, and having pushed off from the land, we awaited the islander's arrival under the branches of a large tree at a little distance from the town.

"Between nine and ten a.m. we heard a number of men singing and keeping time to the motion of many paddles, but we could see no one. However, in a few minutes, a canoe, which was paddled by a few men only, came in sight, and we knew by this that the Water King was approaching. It was instantly followed by another and much larger one, propelled by above twenty very fine young men, whose voices we had been listening to just before, and who were still continuing their song. Their music was slower but very similar to that which may be heard on many parts of the western coast. The King of the Dark Waters was with them. As the canoe drew nearer, we were surprised not only at its extraordinary length and uncommon neatness, but likewise at the unusual display of pomp and show which we observed in her. In the centre a mat awning was erected, which was variously decorated, and on the front of it hung a large piece of scarlet cloth, ornamented with bits of gold lace. In the bow of the canoe were three or four little boys, of equal size, who were clad with neatness and propriety; and in the stern sat a number of comely-looking musicians, consisting of drummers and a trumpeter, while the young men who had the management of the boat were not inferior to their companions either in decency of apparel or respectability of appearance. They all looked, in fact, extremely well."

In spite of rocks, sandbanks, hippopotami, crocodiles and robbers on the banks where they spent their nights, progress was rapid. After some days they reached the confluence of the Benue with the Niger, the spot where Dr Baikie was to settle twenty years later and from which the river was first properly surveyed. Lander thus describes the scene on October 25:

"After five o'clock this morning we found ourselves nearly opposite a very considerable river, entering the Niger from the eastward; it appeared to be three or four miles wide at its mouth, and on the bank we saw a large town, one part of which faced the river and the other the Quorra. We at first supposed it to be the arm of that river and running from us; and therefore directed our course for it. We proceeded up a short distance, but finding the current against us, and that it increased as we got within its entrance, and our people being very tired, we were compelled to give up the attempt, and were easily swept back into the Niger. We conclude this to be the Tshadda, and the large town to be Cuttumcurrafee."

In fact, it was the Benue, "the mother of waters", which they were thus the first to see, but the town near Baikie's settlement at Lokoja is not identifiable, the modern Koton Karifi lying some distance upstream. They were told that the river was called the Tshadda because it flowed from Lake Chad, a journey of nineteen days, though no one had ever attempted it.

At a point a few miles downstream they would have lost their lives, had they not displayed unusual coolness. Having landed to camp, a ferocious band of natives armed with spears and arrows emerged from the woods. Pasko was ordered to the rear to load the muskets while the Landers threw down their pistols to walk composedly towards the leader, who was fitting an arrow to his bow.

"We made all the signs and motions we could with our arms to deter him and his people from firing on us. His quiver was dangling at his side, his bow was bent, and an arrow already trembled on the string when we were within a few yards of his person. This was a highly critical moment – and the next might be our last. But the hand of Providence averted the blow; for just as the chief was about to pull the fatal chord, a man who was nearest to him rushed forward and stayed his arm. At that instant we stood before him and immediately held forth our hands; all of them trembled like aspen leaves; the chief looked up full in our faces, kneeling on the ground – his body convulsed all over and with a timorous expression of countenance, he drooped his head, eagerly grasped our proferred hands, and burst into tears." They had been mistaken for enemies from across the river, but their white faces were so frightening that they were paralysed at the sight. Surely these were the Children of Heaven, dropped out of the skies. All the chief wanted was forgiveness. "That you shall have most heartily," the Landers promised as they shook hands, inwardly thanking God for their escape.

So they continued southward, borne on the smooth waters of a river several miles wide, where there was no sound but the dip of their paddles and the magnificent Niger slumbered in its grandeur. As they approached the forest belt they met the first signs of European influence – a man dressed in the shabby red coat of a soldier, a bottle of rum ("the worst kind of trade rum I have ever tasted"), even a few words of

English picked up from Liverpool vessels trading in the Bonny or Brass rivers.

Such a peaceful voyage did not last long because they were entering the territory of the coastal tribes, which were much more savage than the inhabitants of the Muslim north. As they entered the delta, they were attacked by pirates near Kirree, who plundered their canoe before upsetting it and nearly drowning the brothers in the turmoil of the river battle which followed. A squadron of Ibo canoes, flying flags that looked like Union Jacks, joined in. The white men were stripped naked as they were hauled out of the water, having lost all their possessions except one box that contained John's journal. His account of the disaster is a good example of his narrative style:

"We saw several canoes of amazing size coming towards us from the southward. Totally unsuspicious of danger of any kind from this quarter, astonishment at such a sight was the only emotion which entered my mind; and we resolved to pass in the midst of these canoes for the purpose of ascertaining whether they contained anything belonging to us. At the next moment another squadron of the same description of vessels came in sight, in one of which I could discover my brother by his white shirt, and I fancied that he was returning to demand restitution of the animals of which he had been plundered therefore I still felt perfectly easy in my mind.

"When we drew nearer, it was apparent that these were all war canoes of prodigious dimensions; immense flags of various colours were displayed in them, a six-pounder was lashed to the bow of each; and they were filled with women and children and armed men, whose weapons were in their hands. Such was their size that each of them was paddled by nearly forty people. We passed through the middle of them but could see nothing; and we had advanced a few yards when, on looking behind us, we discovered that the war canoes had been turned round and were swiftly pursuing us. Appearances were hostile; the apprehension of danger suddenly flashed across my mind; we endeavoured and struggled hard to escape; but fear had taken possession of the minds of my companions and as they were unable to exert themselves we were unable to get on; all was vain. Our canoe was overtaken in a moment, and nearly sent under water by the violence with which her pursuer dashed against her; a second crash threw two or three of the Damuggo people overboard, and by the shock of the third she capsized and sunk. All this seemed to be the work of enchantment, so quickly did events succeed each other; yet, in this interval, a couple of ill-looking fellows had jumped into our canoe and in the confusion which prevailed began emptying it of its contents with astonishing celerity.

"On finding myself in the water, my first care was, very naturally, to get out again; and therefore, looking round on a hundred ruffians, in whose countenances I could discern not a single trace of gentleness or pity, I swam to a large canoe, apart from the others, in which I observed two females and some little ones – for in their breasts, thought I, compassion and tenderness must surely dwell. Perceiving my design, a sturdy man of gigantic stature, such as little children dream of, black as coal, and with a most hideous countenance, suddenly sprang towards me, and stooping down he laid hold of my arm and snatched me with a violent jerk out of the water, letting me fall like a log into the canoe, without speaking a word."

Richard and John were now not only prisoners but slaves, without money or even clothes. As such (though with their usual optimism they never accepted the fact) they were sent down river to the king of the Ibos living on the Nun, which is the principal delta river. Richard imagined that his name was Obi, but that was the title of this fantastic little man clad in a scarlet tunic ornamented with gold epaulettes and strings of coral, with tinkling brass anklets. He was vain of his appearance because it denoted the wealth he had obtained from the sale of slaves and palm oil to Europeans, who were not permitted to come up river. The Obi of Ibo welcomed these half-clothed strangers "with infinite cordiality"; none the less, he proposed to sell them to the king of Brass, at the mouth of the river, on the understanding that the latter would demand a ransom from any Liverpool vessel which might be off shore.

There were endless palavers as the brothers awaited their destiny. "We never experienced a more stinging sense of our humbleness and imbecility than on such occasions, and never had we greater need of patience and lowliness of spirit. In most African towns and villages we have been regarded as demi-gods, and treated in consequence with universal kindness, civility and veneration; but here, alas! what a contrast – we are classed with the most degraded and despicable of mankind, and are become slaves in a land of ignorance and barbarism."

Their spirits revived when one of the attendants, a minor chieftain called King Boy, told them that he would convey them on board a brig lying off the mouth of the river, provided a bill on the captain of the ship was paid in return for their freedom. So, in a royal canoe propelled by forty paddles, with a cannon in the bows and a heavily armed crew, they were carried down the last sixty miles of river through dark tunnels of mangroves growing out of the fetid swamp, the smell of which nearly overpowered them. At Brass town, situated on the estuary at the termination of the long-sought Niger, they found the most "wretched, filthy and contemptible place in this world of ours." Governed by a drunken scoundrel called King Jacket, the inhabitants compelled visiting trading ships to employ them as pilots and spent the money thus acquired in consuming vast quantities of the worst rum in the world.

Conducted by King Boy, Richard went on board the

Thomas of Liverpool, while John remained behind as a hostage. The former naturally imagined that their troubles were over, even though he found the brig in sad condition. Four of the crew had just died of fever; four more lay sick in their hammocks, while the captain could hardly walk the deck. Captain Lake turned out to be a "palm oil ruffian" of the worst sort. When Richard asked him to purchase their liberty by paying King Boy,

"... he flatly refused to give a single thing, and ill and weak as he was, made use of the most offensive and shameful oaths I ever heard. 'If you think,' said he, 'that you have a —— fool to deal with, you are mistaken; I'll not give a bloody flint for your bill, I would not give a —— for it.' Petrified with amazement, and horror-struck at such conduct, I shrunk from him in terror. I could scarcely believe what I heard till my ears were assailed by a repetition of the same. Disappointed beyond measure by such brutal conduct from one of my own countrymen, I was ready to sink with grief and shame. I returned to the canoe, undetermined how to act, or what course to pursue."

"Never in my life did I feel such humiliation," as he told King Boy what had happened. The latter's reply was "Dis captain no pay, Bonny captain no pay, I won't take you any further." In desperation, Richard climbed on board the brig once more. In the course of further conversation he mentioned that he had five slaves with him, two of them with experience at sea. Captain Lake at once changed his tune, since he had not enough men to work the ship. He promised to take them on board, but he continued to refuse any payment to King Boy. If the black men of the delta were pirates, the white men who traded with them were rogues.

King Boy's rage when he returned to Brass town without either Richard or payment was such that John's life was in danger. "You are a thief man," he shouted. He had paid the

Obi to free him from slavery. He had brought him down
river. "But you are no good – you are a thief man. Eh!
English captain no will; he no will," stamping on the ground
and grinding his teeth in fury.

Four days later he tried again to obtain payment, this
time bringing John along with him. Richard's anxiety about
the fate of his brother during that time may be imagined,
nor did he receive any sympathy from Lake. "If he had been
alive, he would have been here by this time. Tomorrow
morning I shall leave the river." Surf on the bar prevented
this next day and about midnight, writes Richard, "I saw
several canoes making their way over to the west bank of
the river, in one of which I imagined that I could distinguish
my brother. I observed them soon after land and saw by the
fires which they made that they had encamped under some
mangrove trees. All my fears and apprehensions vanished in
an instant, and I was overjoyed with the thoughts of meeting
my brother in the morning. The captain of the brig, having
observed them, suddenly exclaimed, 'Now we shall have a
little fighting tomorrow; go you and load seventeen muskets
and put five buck shot into each. I will take care that the
cannon shall be loaded to the muzzle with balls and flints,
and if there is any row, I will give them such a scouring as
they never had.' He then directed me to place the muskets
and cutlasses out of sight, near the stern of the vessel, and
said to me, 'The instant that your people come on board,
call them aft, and let them stand by the arms. Tell them if
there is any row, to arm themselves directly and drive all the
Brass people overboard.''

King Boy brought John on board alone. Lake pretended
to be too busy to notice him, whereupon he shouted his
demands for payment. The captain refused, called him "a
black rascal", and threatened to bombard his town if he did
not leave the ship at once. The cheated and disconsolate Boy
climbed over the side and rowed away in his canoe. It is

satisfactory to know that the British authorities later redeemed his debt.

Meanwhile the Landers remained on board, shocked at such dishonesty, for they had paid their way through Africa with scrupulous honesty up to this moment. The next day, November 25, 1830, the brig sailed for Fernando Po, where they bade farewell to the old ruffian.

Clarence Cove, Fernando Po, was now the base for the anti-slave trade patrol in the Bights of Benin and Biafra. It had been leased from the Spanish government in 1827 by Captain W. F. Owen, whose monumental survey of the African coastline was one of the great achievements of the Hydrographical Department in the nineteenth century. The acting Consul was John Beecroft, who became the wisest and most trusted man in the Bights for the next thirty years. He was the only man to survive the lethal climate of the island and to be accepted by the chiefs of the delta; to later explorers of the Niger, he played the part that Warrington had played in the north. A native of Whitby, he had served in both the royal and merchant navies and had travelled in the Arctic before becoming the uncrowned king of this pestiferous place.

Beecroft arranged for the return of the Lander brothers, but it took him months to do so. Having wisely refused a passage home offered by Captain Lake, they found a vessel bound for Rio de Janeiro, where the admiral of the South American station put them on board a transport bound for home. They arrived in England on June 9, 1831.

It is typical of the parsimonious attitude towards this expedition adopted by the Colonial Office that, having paid Richard his £100, John received no *ex gratia* reward whatever. Moreover, a year later we find Richard asking for a pension on the grounds that he was still suffering from fever incurred in their service. He said that his constitution was ruined to such an extent that he was "rendered incapable of

filling any laborious or irksome situation." He asked (as so
many have done) for a prompt reply, "because I am kept in
a state of anxiety and suspense." The pension was refused,
but the Treasury allowed him a Royal Bounty of £100.

The Royal Geographical Society (which Barrow had
founded), on the other hand, awarded him a prize of fifty
guineas, the first of such awards to distinguished explorers.
The occasion was doubly significant because immediately
afterwards the President announced the incorporation of the
African Association with the Society: the Association had
initiated the series of expeditions in search of the Niger which
the Landers had now triumphantly completed; now the
Society was to continue its work by encouraging the exploration of the interior.

The new discoveries compelled even Barrow to change his
mind about the course of the Niger. A naturally generous
man, whose dearest aim was the promotion of discovery in
any part of the world, he now recommended Lander's
journal to John Murray for publication. As Murray's
reader, he had rejected Richard's first narrative on the
grounds that it suffered from "deficiencies of style and sins of
egotism." The truth was that he feared it might compete
with Clapperton's journal, which he himself was editing for
the firm. He now hailed the achievement of the Landers for
what it was and in his review of their narrative he said: "The
long sought for termination of the Niger has now been
discovered, and by a very humble but intelligent individual,
who, without having any theory to support, or prepossession
to gratify set about the task in a straight forward manner,
and accomplished, not without difficulty and danger, an
undertaking in which all former travellers had failed."

Since the great Reform Bill was in the air, together with a
major reorganisation of the Admiralty, for which, as
Secretary, he was chiefly responsible, Barrow had no time
to lick the narratives of Richard and John into shape for

publication. The task of "blending our journals into one" was given to the editor of the *Nautical Magazine*, Lieutenant Becher, whose methods were such that it is now impossible to say which parts were written by Richard and which by John except on stylistic grounds. The book came out in 1832 under the title of *A Journal of an Expedition to Explore the Course and Termination of the Niger* in three duodecimo volumes ornamented by a few crude woodcuts. Always a generous publisher, Murray paid Richard a thousand guineas. The little volumes were translated into many languages, but soon fell out of print until a scholarly selection from the original was brought out in 1965.

Richard Lander's real reward was the inspiration which his discoveries gave to Macgregor Laird, son of the principal Liverpool shipowner trading with Africa. In the conclusion of the brother's journal it was claimed that:

"As we have now ascertained that a water communication may be carried on with an extensive part of the interior of Africa, a considerable trade will be opened with the country through which we have passed. . . . The steam engine, the grandest invention of the human mind, will be a fit means of conveying civilization among these uninformed Africans, who, incapable of understanding such a thing, will view its arrival with astonishment and terror, but will gradually learn to appreciate the benefits they will derive, and to hail its arrival with joy."

It was Macgregor Laird who accepted the challenge, because he agreed that "the splendid discoveries" of the Lander brothers meant that "the long-sought-for highway into Central Africa was at length found."

7

Upstream: Macgregor Laird

In the history of every new found land the trader follows close on the heels of the explorer. Lander having discovered the course of the lower Niger, Liverpool shipowners and merchants were soon planning to exploit a new area where trade, especially in cotton goods, seemed possible. But there were two barriers to the economic development of western and central Africa: the continuance of the slave trade, which hampered legitimate trade at every turn, and the climate, with its attendant diseases. Until these two formidable handicaps were overcome, none of the exploratory trading voyages up the river could possibly succeed.

As a medical historian had written, "The West African coast is equipped with a full range of unpleasant diseases, from sleeping sickness through Guinea worm, bilharzia, yaws, and dysentery, but the principal killers were two, malaria and yellow fever." The mortality of Europeans on the coast at the end of the century is reckoned at anything up to 700 per thousand per annum, largely because the climate favoured the most dangerous type of mosquito and therefore the most fatal form of malaria. As we have seen, the word itself only came into use at the beginning of the nineteenth century, and then as a description of a poisonous exhalation rather than a type of disease. No more poisonous exhalations could be found than those arising in the morning mists from the humid mangrove swamps of the delta, smelling of death and putrefaction.

Hope of a safe return might well be abandoned by those

who were compelled to pass through this region in order to reach the more temperate highlands, which meant in effect the confluence of the Benue with the Niger. This was the goal they invariably aimed at, but few were healthy enough to enjoy its attainment; and there in the savannah country *anopheles gambiae* is actually more at home than in the rain forests. The damage was usually done before the paddle steamers, at an early stage of their development, could make their way up to that point; and when fever struck, there were no remedies beyond the strength of a man's constitution. Cinchona bark was out of fashion, quinine only recently isolated and not yet in general use. Blood letting and mercury treatment were the specifics of the day, fifty ounces of blood at the onset of the illness, or fifty grains of calomel a day to purge and dehydrate were the normal medical practice. The consequence was the evil reputation of the coast as the White Man's Grave. It was under such conditions that Macgregor Laird and later Fowell Buxton launched the first attacks on the Niger problem.

The first attempt to exploit the discoveries made by Richard Lander coincided with the climax of the campaign to abolish slavery in the British dominions in the West Indies, the trade itself having been outlawed many years before. Nevertheless, in Cuba and Brazil the importation of slaves flourished exceedingly and the British anti-slave trade patrol on the West Coast of Africa was far too small to check the illegal activities of the traders. The only hope was to make the trade in legitimate commodities, such as palm oil and cotton goods, sufficiently attractive to ensure that it would replace the trade in "black ivory". It is therefore no accident that Laird's account of his voyage is dedicated to "The Merchants and Philanthropists of Great Britain, in the hope that the attempt recorded in these volumes to establish a Commercial Intercourse with Central Africa, via the River Niger, may open new fields of enterprise to the Mercantile

world, and of usefulness to those who labour for the ameliora-
tion of uncivilised men."

The first writer to imagine how this part of Africa could
be exploited in the search for new markets demanded by an
expanding economy in Britain was a West Indian merchant
named James McQueen, who published his *Geographical and
Commercial View of Northern Central Africa* before the Landers
made their great discovery. In his view, to which Laird and
others later subscribed, civilisation could never be achieved
by native effort alone. "It must be done by a mighty power,
who will take them under its protection until Africa is shown
that it is in the labour and industry of her population, and in
the cultivation of her soil, that true wealth consists. Were we
once established in a commanding attitude on the Niger, the
progress of Improvement will be rapid, and the advantage
great." The history of the last hundred years proves his
point, but when he approached the government in 1820 to
take steps his plans were rejected.

It was with ideas such as these that Macgregor Laird
formed the African Steamship Company with the backing
of a Liverpool merchant, Thomas Stirling, whose name he
gave to a mountain at the confluence of the two rivers where
a trading station was to be established. The company may
have failed in everything it set out to do, but its founder
possessed the faith of a pioneer which was to reap its reward
in the next generation. Laird himself is a fine specimen of
Victorian enterprise, with its thrusting trading habits and
its naïve belief in the benefits of modern science. His lifelong
interest in the development of the African market, whether
by sending steamships up the Niger, or, as later, by building
vessels for Livingstone on the Zambezi, make him the
progenitor of economic imperialism in the best sense of that
much abused phrase.

Not only could Africa be opened up for the purposes of
trade which would in time replace the traffic in human flesh,

but the means of so doing lay to hand in the steamship. He was himself just as interested in the development of the steamship as he was in the future of the oil trade. Palm oil may, indeed, have led him to steam, because its principal use in his day was not soap but as a lubricant for the steam engines which were springing up all over the North of England.

As the revolution in personal hygiene associated with cotton underwear and cold baths progressed in Victorian England, the demand for soap increased, and this is reflected in the figures for the export of palm oil from the Oil Rivers in the delta. Moreover, as this trade began to supplant the age-old trade in slaves from the same area, the regimes which had depended on it for so long were thrown into chaos, creating a situation for the exploitation sought by the palm oil traders. Nevertheless, it was a slow process. For the first fifty years the export of slaves continued at a very high figure and when chiefs were adjured to sign anti-slavery treaties they were apt to be cynical about their validity. As one of the missionaries confessed, "We carried on the slave trade so shortly before ourselves that I do not think they clearly understand why we should be so anxious to suppress it now."

The prosperity of Liverpool no longer depended, as it had in the last century, on the slave trade; nor could the new trade in palm oil be left to the "palm oil ruffians" on the coast. Whereas in 1814 it was stated that only 450 tons of oil was exported from the whole of Africa, by the time Laird came on the scene the figure had increased to 14,000 tons. It was because of this that Laird shared Lander's conviction that the Niger would prove a highway for civilisation, that it would open up "a boundless field of enterprise", and that the new invention of the steamship provided the means of exploiting it.

Macgregor was the younger son of William Laird, the

founder of the famous Birkenhead shipbuilding firm, later known as Cammell Laird. A Scotsman by birth, he was educated at Edinburgh and left his elder brother to carry on the shipbuilding side of the business while he devoted himself to proving the potentiality of the paddle steamer as a means of oceanic transport. The two ships which he chartered for the first Niger expedition were his youthful experiments. Soon after his return he became the leading spirit in the British and North American Steam Navigation Company, which was responsible for chartering the *Sirius* in 1838, the first vessel to cross the Atlantic under continuous steam power. The company's own *British Queen* was not completed in time, but when she was launched she was much larger than her rival, Brunel's *Great Western*, and made regular trans-Atlantic voyages for many years. In 1844 Laird reverted to his interest in West Africa when his own company, the African Steam Ship Company, contracted with the government to send an annual steamer up the Niger, among which the *Rainbow* was the largest paddle steamer of her day. He died in 1861, by which time a regular West African steamship service, as well as a trans-Atlantic line, had been established.

Neither of the ships which sailed for the Niger in 1832 were built by his own firm. The *Quorra*, which was the largest, was a paddle steamer of 145 tons with a 50 h.p. engine, 112' long, 16' broad and drawing only 8' of water – in spite of which she constantly ran aground. She was built by Messrs Fawcett and Preston of Liverpool in the astonishingly short time of two months. More interesting as a pioneering venture was the little 55-ton *Alburkha* (named from the Hausa word for "blessing"), which was the first ocean-going iron ship. She was 70' long, 13' broad. The sailing vessel *Columbine* was chartered as a storeship, but she was never intended to enter the river.

The problem of all steamships before the invention of the

tubular boiler was their enormous consumption of fuel. This
was not so serious at sea, where the engines could be cut off
and the ship proceed under sail, but Laird imagined that
once in the river where sail power was useless, he could
depend on cutting enough logwood on the banks to keep the
engines going. Such had been Captain Marryat's experience
when he used the first steamship in war, the *Diana* of 1823, on
the Irrawaddy. It was only in a calm at sea that the paddles
revolved and Laird gives a good description of the procedure
during the passage out, a procedure which established the
superiority of the steamship over the sailing vessel and gave
rise to the word "liner" for a ship sailing along a regular
route whatever the weather.

"In running down the N.E. Trades we found ourselves
becalmed under the island of Palma though it was ten miles
distant from us: there was a fine breeze about two miles
ahead. The steam was got up, the paddles were connected,
and in ten minutes after the engine was at work we had as
much wind as the vessel would stand. The steam was then
let down, the boilers were blown off, the paddles were
disconnected, and we were under sail again in less than two
hours from the time we had been becalmed."

The expedition was a private venture, the only official
representative on board being Lieutenant William Allen,
whom the Admiralty asked to be allowed to accompany it
in order to make a running survey of the river. The services
of Richard Lander were, of course, invited, and as Richard
was still a young man with no obvious career before him, he
accepted the command of the *Alburkha*. The crew of the
Quorra, when she sailed, was 26 men, that of the *Alburkha* 14,
the Europeans being supplemented (as was the case with all
naval vessels) by Kroomen hired on the coast. The sailing
master of the *Quorra* was Captain Harries, but as he was the
first of the fever casualties, Laird himself had to carry out his
duties with the assistance of a single mulatto engineer. Dr

Briggs, aged twenty-eight, was another early casualty, so that it was the junior surgeon, R. A. K. Oldfield of the *Alburkha*, who wrote the narrative of that ship. Both vessels were armed with small swivel guns and protected (at Lander's insistance) by *chevaux de frise* running along the bulwarks in order to prevent hostile natives climbing on board.

The two ships sailed from Milford Haven on 25 June 1832, because of a cholera epidemic at Liverpool. Their first port of call in West Africa was Freetown, Sierra Leone, where a number of Kroomen were hired. These admirable seamen had long been valued by captains of warships because of their loyalty and good discipline (imposed by one of their own number, never by a European), as well as their remarkable ability as seamen. Since their native names were unpronounceable, they were called by such nicknames as After Dinner, Pea Soup or Bottled Beer.

At Cape Coast Castle they stayed with Governor Maclean, the real founder of the Gold Coast colony, though at that date his rule was confined to the old fort itself. He was the husband of the popular Victorian poetess L.E.L., in whose mysterious death by poisoning he was supposed to be implicated, though in fact it seems to have been a case of an accidental dose of prussic acid. Here Lander met his old friend Pasko for the third time, together with his ex-slave Judy. Both signed on for the voyage.

At the mouth of the Nun the first fever casualties occurred – Captain Harries, the sailing master, and the boatswain of the *Alburkha*. There they found the brig *Susan* from Liverpool with half her crew dead, having been immobilised at that deadly spot for the past seven months for want of hands to work the ship. It was an ominous introduction to Africa.

A black pilot took the ships over the bar, where they met King Boy once more. Lander's reaction on renewing acquaintance with the man who had been cheated so

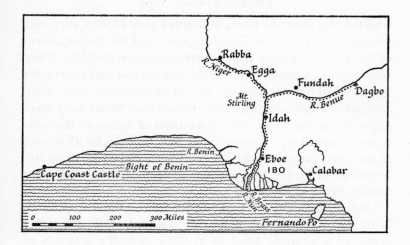

scandalously is not known, but Laird gives a fantastic description of his appearance: "A Highland uniform, which had been sent out to him by my father, consisting of a red coat, full dress kilt and yellow slippers; the whole surmounted by a military hat, with a feather in it about a yard long." Not surprisingly, his reception of Lander and his friends was cool, though he insisted on following the steamers in his royal canoe with the intention (Laird suspected) of arranging ambushes when members of the crew went on shore to cut wood. He had sold Lander's journal to the captain of the *Susan* and the manuscript thus came into Lander's hands again, but it was subsequently lost.

Surgeon Oldfield, whose trivial narrative was printed along with Laird's, was left behind in the *Columbine* with nothing to do but watch Spanish slavers loading a cargo for Cuba. He, too, went down with fever, but recovered.

The serpentine course of the delta river made progress slow through the swamps. Laird had awnings stretched over the deck to protect his men from the ill effects of dews and exhalations, but the device merely increased the airless heat

133

which hung over the river. Wherever they landed they met Africans suffering from horrible ulcers and the consequences of the Guinea worm, which burrows under the skin. They were an idle, unhealthy lot, subsisting on fish and vegetables imported from further up the river because they were incapable of growing anything themselves. What they most enjoyed was imbibing "vast quantities of spirits of the very worst description." Lander, who had no love for that part of the river, imagined plots at every turn and wrote dramatic warnings to Laird, but nothing materialised beyond some aimless firing of muskets.

Once into the country of the Ibos, everything improved. King Obie (as Laird, following Lander, calls the Obi) occupied a strategic position at Eboe near the junction of the delta rivers Nun, Bonny and Benin. As before, he was festooned with coral necklaces and just as insistent that slave trading paid better than palm oil. He was an impressive figure, over six foot tall. An elaborately staged ceremonial visit was duly paid.

"The launch and other boats were manned by Kroomen, dressed in kilts and velvet caps, an uniform expressly intended for gala days; and at 10 a.m. we proceeded in state to pay our respects to the king. Mr Lander in a general's uniform, with a feather in his cocked hat that almost reached the ground; Mr Jordan in a colonel's uniform, and Lieutenant Allen in his own, led the van and attracted so much of the natives' attention that Dr Briggs and myself almost regretted that we had not visited Monmouth Street before our departure from England."

Though the scenery improved after they left "the accursed swamps" behind them, fever continued to take its toll. There were thirteen deaths on board the *Quorra*, ten on the *Alburkha*. Lander, as yet in good health, proved an excellent liaison officer with the inhabitants until he, too, with Lieutenant

Allen, succumbed, while Laird, after recovering from his first attack, found himself too weak to stand.

The confluence of the Niger with the Benue was reached at last, after two months on the river, and only half a ton of ivory to show for it. Nevertheless, Laird established a warehouse for his goods, though this first trading post in the interior of Africa never came to anything. It was a building situated 250' up the square-topped mountain which they called Mount Stirling, dominating the junction of the two rivers. There was deep water nearby, but the *Quorra* managed to run aground once more and remained immobile on a sandbank for several weeks. As all who saw the place testified, the scenery at the spot where the seeds of British rule in Nigeria were sown was magnificent beyond words:

"An immense river, about a thousand yards wide, extending as far as the eye could reach, lay before us, flowing majestically between its banks, which rose gradually to a considerable height and were studded with clumps of trees and brushwood, giving them the appearance of a gentleman's park; while the smoke rising from the different towns on its banks, and the number of canoes floating on its bosom, gave it an aspect of security and peace far beyond any African scene I had yet witnessed. The confluence of the Shary was just in sight, and a range of low hills on the northern bank trended north-east; while on the western bank of the Niger were two remarkable isolated table-lands of a romantic and beautiful appearance."

After allowing time to recover the health of the crew, it was intended that Lander in the *Alburkha* should proceed up to Rabba, while Laird in the *Quorra*'s longboat (the ship being still aground) should explore the Shary or Tchadda, as the Benue was then called. To pass away the monotony of the waiting interval, Laird set up a market on land, but few people attended it and his depression was deepened by the death of his closest friend, Dr Briggs.

Nothing is recorded about the *Alburkha*'s voyage, because Lander kept no journal. Laird, however, describes in detail his visit to Fundah, some thirty miles north of the Benue, which he reached partly by longboat, partly by canoe, partly by hammock, since he was too weak to stand. The King of Fundah, a Muslim, had an evil reputation, having poisoned two brothers to secure the throne and driven a third to suicide. Contact having been made with him, an embassy returned from the king in the shape of eighteen magnificent horsemen, who knelt down before the Liverpool merchant and placed his foot upon their heads before delivering a message of welcome.

The inhabitants of Fundah had never seen a white man, so that Laird, lying sick in his hammock, was pestered with their attentions. He found the king splendidly dressed, but "his countenance is by no means prepossessing, particularly his eyes, which are of a dirty red colour, having a sinister and foreboding expression." Laird presented him with the usual swords, pistols and umbrella, but as the days passed and Laird lay in his verminous hut, promises turned to altercations, altercations to threats of poisoning and a total refusal to trade. Poor Laird had by now contracted craw-craw from his Kroomen, a virulent type of scabies which produced a maddening itch developing into ulcers.

After a week of this he sent a messenger back to the ship. He returned with the news that Lander has sent the *Alburkha* downstream and was himself on the way down in a canoe. But the messenger also brought back some Congreve rockets. When these were fired off they made such an impression that Laird, now virtually a prisoner, was permitted to leave the town. As earlier explorers had found, there was nothing like a display of fireworks to act as an effective ju-ju.

Young Surgeon Oldfield, who brought the *Alburkha* back upstream again, met Lander on his way down. "On asking how was Dr Briggs? his reply was 'Dead' – how was Mr

Laird? 'Very ill and not expected to recover' – how was Captain Miller? 'Dead' – Mr Jordan? – 'Dead'. In short, officers and men were almost all dead." Lander himself was too ill to stand, so that Oldfield was worn out looking after him day and night. But by the time they returned to the confluence, and Laird had returned from Fundah, they recovered a little. Unfortunately, the cheerful rogue Pasko, Lander's companion for so long, met his end when he was poisoned by a local chief for advising the white men to trade further north and showing them the way thither.

The rains now set in. Uncomfortable as were the accompanying tornadoes, the crews of both ships recovered their spirits when the *Quorra* floated off her sandbank as the water rose and Laird decided to take her downstream on the flood. The ever-enterprising Lander and Allen took the *Alburkha* a short way up the Benue on another futile visit to Fundah and then continued further in order to find out if the river was really connected with Lake Chad, as the natives asserted. The further they got, the wilder the country and the more savage the inhabitants. At a collection of beehive huts called Dagbo news reached them that the king of Bornou would not welcome any further progress. Lander, still suffering from dysentery, was glad of an excuse to return.

Back at Fernando Po, Laird recovered his health sufficiently to accompany Colonel Nicolls, the Governor, on a visit to Duke Ephraim, the ruler of the notorious slaving port of Old Calabar. The savagery of the delta tribes on the Nun had been bad enough, but it was nothing to that of the inhabitants of the Calabar: "I was much struck by the extreme demoralisation and barbarism of the inhabitants, in comparison with the natives of the interior. The human skulls that are seen in every direction, and that are actually kicking about the streets, attest the depravity of feeling among the people, and add another to the long list of melancholy proofs of the debasing effects of European intercourse with savage nations, when governed solely by the love of gain."

Partly as a result of conversations with Nicolls and Beecroft (who was to be his successor as consul on the island), partly because of its obvious geographical advantages, Laird became an enthusiast for the retention of Fernando Po by the British government. Though nominally under Spanish sovereignty, the English were the only Europeans on the island, using Clarence Cove as a watering base for ships on the anti-slavery patrol. To Laird, the place seemed "the key to Central Africa." It was not as unhealthy as it was reputed to be, certainly not as bad as the delta, and as a base for steamship navigation it offered great advantages, provided the government took the place seriously and spent money on improving its facilities.

Colonel Edward Nicolls naturally agreed with Laird about the importance of the island, but two years later he was ordered to resign as Governor, though a consulate was continued there for some time. Nicolls also became Laird's son-in-law. He was an interesting man, nicknamed "Fighting Nicolls" from his long service as an officer in the Royal Marines. Before coming to Fernando Po, he had commanded the garrison at the island of Ascension and in both places left behind him a fine record of improving the amenities of the place for those unfortunate men engaged in the anti-slavery patrol. He himself initiated the policy of negotiating anti-slavery treaties with local chiefs, but the government usually refused to ratify them because it feared that they would involve this country in a part of Africa which was not then in favour. Beecroft, his successor, continued the same policy in an even more energetic way and the two men seem to have been the only Englishmen who ever liked that unhealthy part of the world. All the explorers from the south were indebted to them for their encouragement and hospitality, as those from the north were indebted to Warrington, the consul at Tripoli, and life would have been much easier for them had the Colonial Office listened to their advice about annexing this island.

Laird left Fernando Po for Liverpool in October, 1833. He never entirely recovered his health after his experience in Africa, but he continued to devote himself to the task of promoting the development of steam navigation to that continent. The others – Lander, Allen and Oldfield – still had a year of activity before them. Once more they got as far as Rabba in the *Alburkha*, where trouble with a cylinder prevented them from going on to Bussa. Returning downstream, they heard of Laird's departure for home and decided that Allen, too, should return with his survey. It was a rough chart, but it had to serve for another twenty years before the course of the lower Niger was properly surveyed by Lieutenant Glover; nor could any chart be accurate for long, so quickly did the sandbanks shift after every rainy season.

Lander then decided to go to Cape Coast Castle for a supply of cowries, the currency of the Niger tribes, leaving Oldfield to take the little steamer upstream again. He promised to join him in six weeks' time, but Oldfield never saw him again.

The *Alburkha* ran aground before she reached Eboe, so that Oldfield had to ask the king for the loan of four canoes and a number of "pullaboys" in order to tow her off, as well as a quantity of butter to serve as a lubricant. When he returned to the ship on the last day of the year, he found that the only surviving white engineer had died and that the mate was suffering from *delirium tremens*. The young man now found himself performing the duties of doctor, engineer and commander of the remaining Kroomen.

In spite of this, in spite of the fact that the ship was constantly running aground, that her stern anchor was lost and her running rigging was falling to pieces after the rains, he pressed on up the river. On March 29, 1834, he received Lander's last letter, dated January 22:

"Dear Sir, Having an opportunity of writing to you by King Boy, who will give it to King Obie to forward to you, I avail myself of it. I was coming up to you with a cargo of cowries and dry goods worth £400 when I was attacked from all quarters by the natives of Hyammah, eighty-four miles above the Nun. The shots were very numerous, both from the island and the shore. . . . I am wounded, but I hope not dangerously, the ball having entered close to the anus and struck the thigh bone: It is not extracted yet. . . . We are now under weigh for Fernando Po. I remain your most affectionate friend, R. L. Lander."

Lander was never much of a hand at expressing himself on paper, but Oldfield was relieved to hear that the wound was apparently not serious. However, on Lander's return to Fernando Po mortification set in and on about 7 February (the exact date has never been ascertained) he died. Oldfield heard the news in a curiously phrased letter from Colonel Nicolls, warning him to beware of another ambush, but as the letter, dated April 24, did not reach him for three months, the warning was useless.

"Dear Sir, You will no doubt be much annoyed at hearing that Mr Lander died of the wounds he received in an attack that was made upon him in a most treacherous manner by the natives of Hyammah. I am in hopes that this may reach you at Eboe, as it will put you on your guard. As you pass, keep well in the centre of the river and, if possible, steam quickly past them. . . . To Surgeon Oldfield, or the Officer in Charge of the African Inland Company's Affairs in the River Niger. Believe me to be truly yours, Edward Nicolls, Lieutenant-Colonel Commander and Superintendent, on board the *Quorra*, in the Nun, April 24, 1835."

By the time he received the letter, Oldfield was back in the

Nun after a fruitless attempt to trade further north. "Poor Lander," he wrote, "he fell a victim to his too great confidence in the natives." He was convinced that the Obi was behind the attack, but this does not seem to have been the truth. An unarmed canoe laden with trade goods was an open invitation to an attack on that lawless stretch of river. Lander was in no position to repel boarders. He was unarmed, weak after several months of dysentery, and without any white companion to support him. Like Mungo Park, the discoverer of the upper Niger, and at about the same age, the discoverer of the lower Niger died from wounds received at Angiama on the river at the hands of its inhabitants.

When Oldfield moored the *Alburkha* alongside the *Quorra* at Clarence Cove the sad tale of the mortality suffered during the two years the ships had spent on the river could be told. Excluding the Kroomen, twenty-four persons died on board the *Quorra*, Laird, Allen, the purser and two seamen being the only Europeans to survive. On board the *Alburkha* there were fifteen deaths, Oldfield and one seaman surviving. Only nine of the forty-eight Europeans who left England returned. The two steamers were left to rot at Clarence Cove.

In spite of this appalling toll and his own continuing ill health, Macgregor Laird had nothing to say about the disease factor when he summed up the lessons learned on this first attempt to trade on the Niger. Instead, he drew up an optimistic programme for the future, which Fowell Buxton was to elaborate in a more widely read book published two years later, and which in turn led to another and equally fatal effort to exploit the area. In both cases the object was the same: to replace the trade in slaves with that in palm oil.

Quite apart from the moral evils of the slave trade, which, though long since outlawed by most states on both sides of the Atlantic, was running at a rate far in excess of the numbers transported when the trade was legal, Laird showed how its continued existence prevented the growth of any other sort of economic activity. It paid so well that as soon as the slave ships appeared at the mouth of one of the delta rivers, all trade with other vessels stopped immediately, because every effort was made to load human cargoes from the "barracoons", or barracks where slaves were kept, as quickly as possible. At any moment a British cruiser might appear. Only when such loading was completed could legitimate trade be resumed.

Despite such handicaps, British trade with West Africa had doubled over the past seven years, so that it now amounted to five times the trade with Sweden, double that with the Levant. Imports from the coast were valued at over £1 million, of which palm oil accounted for half, gold dust, ivory and teak timber for the remainder. Is it not, asked Laird, the economic as well as the moral duty of the government to promote such a valuable trade by suppressing that in slaves? Most people would agree, but the problem was how to do it. In Laird's view, slavery should be categorised as piracy. Under American law this was the case, but that did not stop Baltimore shipbuilders selling clippers to Cuban importers, nor did it increase the activity of the handful of U.S. Navy ships which occasionally appeared off the coast, though never in the Bight of Benin. The task of interception was left to the dozen or so gunbrigs of the Royal Navy composing the West Africa Squadron. Laird suggested tighter blockade methods, but this was impossible without vastly increasing the expenditure on the squadron. In the early thirties there was much to be said for his assertion that British cruising policy merely aggravated the sufferings of slaves by compelling their shippers to use small, fast clippers in which cargoes were packed as tightly as was humanly possible:

"By our present system we have made the slave trade a

smuggling one, and instead of large and commodious vessels which it would be in the interest of the slave trader to employ we have, by our interference, forced him to use a class of vessels (well known to naval men as American clippers) of the very worst description that could be imagined for the purpose, every quality being sacrificed for speed. . . . Aware as I am of the baleful effects the trade produces throughout the whole continent of Africa, I would prefer seeing it legalised rather than the present ineffectual system of prevention should be continued.''

It was a counsel of despair which it was fortunate that Whig Foreign Secretaries in the next decade, such as Palmerston and Russell, refused to accept. Laird failed to see that the problem was a diplomatic one, involving Right of Search treaties with all the major powers, as well as local treaties with native chiefs which could only be negotiated or imposed by increasing the number of naval vessels in the squadron. In fact, by spending a lot more money on the task of suppression than had hitherto been the case.

He was scarcely more realistic in his proposals for promoting legitimate trade, though long after he was dead, when a different climate of opinion prevailed, the steps taken in what was to become Nigeria by such empire-builders as Goldie and Lugard were in many ways similar to those he proposed fifty years earlier for very different reasons. He wanted the establishment of a chain of trading posts, garrisoned by local levies paid by the British government, stretching all the way up the Niger as far as Timbuktu, with a supply base at Fernando Po. He never used the word "factories," but the armed warehouses which he contemplated were similar to those long established by the East India Company; nor did he have the historical imagination to see how inevitably these developed into colonial outposts. Territorial aggrandisement of any kind was far from his mind. Yet he speaks in twentieth-century language about the desirability of educating an élite by establishing schools and offering scholarships to those who wished to study medicine or engineering in Britain. When, a century later, such a policy was adopted, the favourite subject was law and the result was the creation of African nationalism, not, as he hoped, the extension of British influence.

When he wrote, in the year in which Queen Victoria came to the throne, civilisation was equated with European (preferably British) morality and technology. To export this to a benighted continent was ever his wider aim, not only the promotion of trade or the employment of steamships. Lander had claimed that the Niger would be a highway of civilisation. Laird agreed, and showed how the steamship might be the instrument. Such was the vision which exhilarated his prose:

"British influence and enterprise would thereby penetrate into the remotest recesses of the country, one hundred millions of people would be brought into direct contact with the civilised world; new and boundless markets would be opened to our manufacturers; a continent teeming with inexhaustible fertility would yield her riches to our traders; not merely a nation, but hundreds of nations, would be awakened from the lethargy of centuries, and become useful and active members of the great commonwealth of mankind; and every British station would become a centre from whence religion and commerce would radiate their influence into the surrounding country. Who can calculate the effect that would be produced if such a plan were followed out, and Africa, freed from her chains moral and physical, allowed to develop her energies in peace and security?"

The means lay to hand in the legacy of "the immortal Watt":

"By his invention every river is laid open to us, time and distance are shortened. If his spirit is allowed to witness the success of his invention here on earth, I can conceive no application of it that would meet his approbation more than seeing the mighty streams of the Mississippi and the Amazon, the Niger and the Nile, the Indus and the Ganges, stemmed by hundreds of steam-vessels, carrying the glad tidings of 'peace and good will towards men' into the dark places of the earth which are now filled with cruelty."

8

The Second Attempt:
Allen and Trotter

The formidable store of moral energy generated by the Nonconformist and Evangelical conscience at the beginning of the century in the crusade to abolish slavery within the British dominions began to be directed towards missionary activity overseas when that objective had been achieved. As the continent of Africa was opened up piece by piece by the explorers, it attracted most of the attention of the innumerable philanthropic and missionary societies which were accustomed to meet in Exeter Hall. The illegal slave trade, however, remained active in both West and East Africa, so that, as Livingstone's career was to show, the work of the explorer-missionary was inextricably bound up with the older requirement to eradicate a trade which, whether carried on by Portuguese or by Arab traders in the Atlantic or the Indian oceans, remained the principal stumbling block to the moral and economic development of the continent.

As befitted the dominant sea power, Britain shouldered the main burden of the task of suppression by sea. Ever since the abolition of the extensive British trade in 1807, cruisers of the West African Squadron based on Sierra Leone or the island of Ascension operated on the slave coast in order to intercept the vessels of illegal traders exporting negroes to Cuba or Brazil. Such men were predominantly of Portuguese or Spanish nationality. They used American-built vessels and sailed under any false colours which might delude efforts to stop and search them: one even flew the flag of the Papal States. Their ships were such fast sailers that the over-gunned brigs employed to chase them had small chance of success, nor was the Admiralty ever enthusiastic about implementing such philanthropic work in the worst climate in the world. Just how unimportant the Squadron was in the eyes of their Lordships may be judged from the fact that it was under the orders of the Commander-in-Chief of the Cape of Good Hope, a station which covered the enormous area between Mozambique on the east coast to Cape Verde on the west. In the abstract of ships employed on foreign stations in 1840, there were 14 ships on this Cape and West Africa station, 26 on the North American and West Indies, 23 on the Mediterranean.

The consequence of employing so few and such unsuitable ships against the slavers was that the number of negroes exported annually from West Africa rose (even though the trade was illegal) from an estimated 85,000 in 1810 to 135,000 in 1840. Of these, only 2,374 were actually liberated from vessels captured at sea that year. As Laird complained, naval efforts to suppress the slave trade were obviously as futile as earlier efforts to stop smuggling.

The division of opinion in England as to the best remedy to eradicate this shameful state of affairs was complex and paradoxical. While Palmerston, Russell and the Whigs traditionally favoured the cause of suppression, they were at the same time encouraging slave-grown sugar by their economic policies. Members of the Society of Friends, always in the van of the abolitionist movement, found themselves in the pacifist's dilemma: which was worse, supporting slavers or encouraging naval officers to suppress them by force? When Joseph Sturge, a leading Quaker emancipationist, founded the British and Foreign Anti-Slavery Society in 1839, the result, if not the avowed aim, was to oppose the use of force in suppressing the traffic.

It is to the credit of Sir Thomas Fowell Buxton, the accredited successor of Wilberforce in the cause of emancipation, that he accepted the necessity of increasing expenditure on the Squadron; but as he was closely connected with the Quakers by marriage he had to apologise to his relations for so doing in the preface of his influential book, *The African Slave Trade and its Remedy* (1840). He had been responsible for introducing the final bill of emancipation in the House of Commons in 1833, but having now retired after many years as a Member of Parliament, he devoted himself to the cause of suppressing the illegal slave trade by founding the Society for the Extinction of the Slave Trade and for the Civilisation of Africa in the same year as Sturge's Society. It was a much more high-powered body, consisting of representatives of the nobility, together with a number of bishops and Members of Parliament, who were guided by the principle that "the only complete cure for these evils is the introduction of Christianity into Africa." The means advocated were the strengthening of the Squadron, the encouragement of native agriculture and the promotion of legitimate trade on the Niger.

Significantly, the name of Macgregor Laird is absent from the list of members. The book which Buxton wrote only two years after Laird's recommendations were made never refers to them and only mentions his expedition in passing. Whereas Laird had been drawn to the Niger by commercial, as well as philanthropic motives, Buxton proposed "to raise the native mind" by a policy of Christianisation. Whereas Laird's expedition was a private venture, Buxton had the official backing of the Colonial Office, the Admiralty and the Treasury, which footed the bill. Whereas Laird's was a minor failure, Buxton's was a major disaster.

His approach to the problem of opening up Africa was singularly naïve. He was convinced by the narratives of Clapperton and Lander that native chiefs would welcome settlements on the banks of the Niger, because he took the facile promises of Sultan Bello and the King of Wawa at their face value. The psychological antipathy of the African male towards manual labour, and, more important, the deadly effects of the climate were disregarded, so that the lessons of Laird's failure were ignored. Citing the questionable precedent of the colony at Sierra Leone for liberated slaves, Buxton proposed "that an effort be made to cultivate districts of Africa, in order that her inhabitants may be convinced of the capabilities of her soil, and witness what wonders may be accomplished by their own labours when set in motion by our capital and guided by our skill." The site for the initial experiment was to be the confluence of the Niger with the Benue, though the reader is never reminded that this was Laird's choice: "this position will, hereafter, become the great internal citadel of Africa, and the great emporium of her commerce." No wonder that when William Allen (now a Captain in the Navy, a Fellow of the Royal Society and of the Geographical Society) was asked his opinion, he replied: "I find embodied in the book all the ideas I had formed on the same subject."

With the blessing of old Thomas Clarkson (now living in retirement from his labours in the Lake District), Buxton approached members of the Cabinet and at a meeting with Lord John Russell, the Colonial Secretary, and Lord Minto, the First Lord of the Admiralty, on 10 September, 1839, it was agreed that the Treasury should be approached to defray the expenses and that the Admiralty should provide three steam vessels. Buxton also wanted the government to acquire sovereignty of any area ceded under treaty with a local ruler, but the Colonial Office refused to entertain the idea of a colony, fearing that it would involve this country in tribal squabbles. James Stephen, the formidable civil servant in that department, stated flatly that no colony was wanted in Africa.

Preparations for an official expedition to the Niger now

went forward. The commanders of the three vessels were appointed – H. Dundas Trotter, William Allen and Bird Allen, all of them experienced naval surveyors and in William Allen's case a man who had charted and navigated the river itself. They were sent on a tour of the north of England to hire suitable steamers, but without success. Sir Edward Parry, late Hydrographer of the Navy and a distinguished Arctic explorer, was therefore asked to specify the type of vessel required which was to be fitted out by Laird's firm. Two identical vessels were ordered, with another smaller one to accompany them as a storeship. All were iron-hulled paddle steamers, square-rigged fore and aft, with 35 h.p. engines. The *Albert* and *Wilberforce* measured 139' by 27', 457 tons each, the *Soudan* 113' by 22', 249 tons. They were flat-bottomed to ensure a shallow draught, so that keelboards had to be fitted for the ocean voyage. They were sub-divided with water-tight compartments in case of damage to the hull by grounding, and because they were constructed of iron the Astronomer Royal devised two powerful bar magnets to counteract the consequent deviation of the compass.

Their most remarkable feature was an enormous iron chest or filter on the upper deck, through which tubes passed to ventilate the lower deck. This contraption was invented by Dr Reid, who had been responsible for the ventilation of the new House of Commons. He called it a "medicator", because he imagined it as a filter for the deadly miasmata thought to be the cause of fever and for what he called "vitiated air", i.e. carbon dioxide. In practice, the thing was found to take up far too much deck space and almost asphyxiated the unfortunate seamen who slept below in the torrid atmosphere of an equatorial night.

Each ship carried a surgeon. In the event, it was the surgeon of the *Albert*, Dr J. O. MacWilliam, who brought the "plague ship filled with the dead or dying" back to safety in the Bight of Benin, because all the other officers were dead or incapacitated. His medical history of the expedition was published separately, whereas the journal of Surgeon W. M. Pritchett of the *Wilberforce*, with its fifty-page treatise on what he called *febris africanus* – "the extraordinary and devastating malady which unhappily caused the breaking up of the expedition almost immediately on reaching the field of its labours" – remains a dusty, yellowing relic in the Public Record Office. Pritchett had the good sense to doubt the miasmatic theory of causation – "an hypothesis about to be exploded, which has hitherto hung like an incubus on the shoulders of truth" – but could only replace it with "solar exposure" and treat the disease with cupping, calomel and castor oil. He tried quinine in wine as a prophylactic, but found it useless in the early stages: "probably the best means will be found of simply endeavouring to assist Nature in her efforts to overcome the morbid action, instead of attempting to take the enemy by storm."

Thompson, the surgeon of the *Soudan*, who contributed much of the natural history in Trotter and Allen's published narrative, was of the opinion that "quinine acted more like a specific than anything else": "from subsequent experience, we believe that if used boldly and in full doses, it may be used beneficially at a much earlier stage." As to causation, he thought that at the end of the rainy season there was "a certain peculiarity of atmosphere – call it miasm, malaria or any other name – which, though inappreciable by chemical agency, operates most powerfully on Europeans." He himself took 6–8 grains daily as a prophylactic. All three surgeons survived – perhaps the dosage given to others was insufficient. Certainly, Captain Trotter was not to blame, because he ordered that it should be given "occasionally, and its issue may be extended to the whole crew when thought desirable by the surgeons." Unfortunately, there is insufficient medical evidence to explain exactly why the 1841 expedition was a disaster, whereas that its successor in 1854 was a success.

While preparations for the expedition were being made, Beecroft, now consul at Fernando Po, had been collecting information about the delta rivers, which sailors now called the Gate of the Cemetery. He knew nothing about what was happening at home, but during the past few years he had explored the delta on his own account. In 1836 he and Surgeon Oldfield had taken Duke Ephraim 120 miles up the Calabar river in the old *Quorra*, thinking that it might be one of the mouths of the Niger. Back in London, Allen disproved this in a paper read to the Geographical Society, though he admitted there might be some connection via the river Cross. Then Robert Jamieson, a Liverpool merchant and philanthropist like Laird, presented him with a little paddle steamer called the *Ethiope*. With fifteen Europeans and Lander's old interpreter, Beecroft entered the Bonny-Benin mouth, but he had to cut his way through the vegetation which almost blocked the stream. He reached Rabba and might have gone on to Bussa had not the rapids defeated his 30 h.p. engine. On this six-month voyage he showed that the river was only navigable at certain times of the year and that, therefore, in his opinion, it was of negligible commercial value.

A previous visitor to the ill-famed city of Benin, later known as the City of Blood, came to the same conclusion, though his narrative was only printed quite recently. This was R. M. Jackson, surgeon of the Liverpool trader *Kingston* in 1826. He describes the climate as "most sickly and pernicious to Europeans. Diseases of a Dysenteric and Febrifuge nature are easily imbibed from the Miasma (or 'Smokes') that constantly arise from marshes contiguous to the Town."

Jamieson's and Beecroft's little steamer was to play a vital part in the Buxton expedition as the tug which towed the fever-stricken *Albert* out of trouble. Had Buxton relied more

Lieutenant
John Glover R.N.

The *Dayspring* bringing supplies to Baikie at Lokoja

The Confluence of the rivers Niger and Chadda; from W. Allen
Descriptive View of the Niger 1840

Dr Heinrich Barth

Dr. W. B. Baikie: from an obituary notice in the *Illustrated London News*

The *Quorra* aground near Lokoja. From an engraving by Westall after a sketch by Macgregor Laird

on Beecroft's knowledge of the area, the story of the expedition for which he was responsible (he was too ill to take any part in it) might have been happier. Meanwhile his main objectives were set out in the Colonial Secretary's instructions to the leaders, who were called Commissioners because they were empowered to negotiate treaties. They were reminded that "they must always bear in mind that the main object of your Commission is the extinction of the Foreign Slave Trade, and all other points must for the present be considered subordinate." Such points included Buxton's favourite panacea, the establishment of a Model Farm. "It is considered desirable by H.M. Government to have power to erect one or more small Forts on the Niger, from whence to watch over the due execution of the agreements to assist in the abolition of the Slave Trade, and to protect and further the innocent trade of H.M. subjects. . . . The establishment of a position near to the confluence of the rivers Niger and Tchadda would have the additional advantage of assisting the British trade with both rivers."

The three ships sailed from England in May, 1841. Trotter commanded the *Albert*, William Allen the *Wilberforce* and Bird Allen the *Soudan*. The white crews totalled 135 men, to which a further 133 coloured seamen were added, either as volunteers at home or as Kroomen recruited at Sierra Leone. In addition to the executive officers, there were chaplains and surgeons, a botanist, a mineralogist, a geologist and a West Indian called Mr Carr ("a gentleman of colour") to superintend the agricultural experiment. At Sierra Leone, at the request of the Church Missionary Society, two missionaries joined, whose accounts of the expedition were the first to be printed. One was the Rev. J. F. Schön, who proved useful as an interpreter, and the other was a negro, Samuel Crowther.

Crowther was to become the first Bishop of the Niger. His story was a romantic one. At the age of eleven he was taken as a slave from his village on the middle Niger. The vessel which was to have carried him to Cuba was intercepted by a ship of the West African Squadron commanded by Captain H. J. Leake in 1822. He was baptised and brought up with other liberated slaves at Sierra Leone and when, in old age, he was consecrated Bishop at Canterbury Cathedral Captain Leake was in the congregation at the ceremony. Trotter describes him at the age of fifty-three as "an intelligent and well-educated native", but his subsequent career as the first African missionary shows that he was much more than that.

The date on which the ships crossed the bar of the Nun – Friday, August 13 – was not auspicious. The first ruler with whom they had any dealings was the Obi of Ibo at Aboh (Lander's Eboe). Trotter was the first to discover that Obi was his title and that his full name was Ezzek Obi Osai. He also discovered much else at this unsavoury court: the infanticide of twins, for instance, and that of any child which cut its first teeth on the upper jaw. The ideal of feminine beauty was the same as among the Arabs:

"The Ibu women are famed for their charms, and in order to heighten them, when a man takes a wife, his first care is to immure her in a hut, without suffering her to take exercise, until she attains the acme of beauty, according to the Ibu taste, such an amount of obesity as very materially to interfere with the faculty of locomotion."

Negotiating a treaty with the Obi was a farcical business. The conversation of the Commissioners through an inter- preter on board the *Albert* was reported verbatim:

Commissioners: Does Obi sell slaves from his own domin- ions?

Obi: No; they come from countries far away.

Commissioners: Does Obi make war to procure slaves?

Obi: When other chiefs quarrel with me and make war, I take all I can as slaves. . . . I will agree to discontinue the slave trade, but I expect the English to bring goods for traffic.

Commissioners: The Queen's subjects cannot come here to trade unless they are certain of a proper supply of your produce.

Obi: I have plenty of palm oil. I made you a promise to drop this slave trade, and do not wish to hear anything more about it.

But the catechism went on relentlessly.

Commissioners: Wicked white men come and buy slaves; not to eat them, as your people believe, but to make them work harder than they can bear by flogging and ill using them. The English Queen wishes to prevent such cruelty.

Obi: I believe everything you say, and I once more consent to give up the slave trade.

Gifts were brought in, which was all the Obi bothered about, but the questions continued and he began snapping his fingers with impatience.

Commissioners: If the Queen makes a treaty with Obi, will his successors, on his death, abide by the same?

Obi: They will do as I command. I am tired of so much talking and wish to go on shore.

Worse followed when the treaty was actually signed. The Rev. Schön began to say some prayers. Everyone kneeled down, including the Obi.

"He soon became violently agitated. On the conclusion of the ceremony he started up, and, uttering a fearful exclamation, called aloud for his ju-ju man to bring his protecting idol, being evidently under the impression that we had performed some incantation to his prejudice. He stood trembling with fear and agitation, the perspiration streaming down his face, showing how great was the agony of mind he endured. The priest had heard the cry of his sovereign and rushing into the cabin with the idol – a piece of blackened wood enveloped in a cloth – which the King placed between his feet, was about to offer the customary libation of palm wine when Captain Trotter, also much disconcerted at the idea of a heathen ceremony being performed in our presence and in opposition to the rites of our holy religion, interrupted him and called for Captain Bird Allen. It was an interval of breathless anxiety, the King becoming every moment more alarmed and desirous to continue his sacrifice, till it was explained to him that we had asked the Great God, who was Father of us all, to bestow his blessing on the black people and on us. This immediately pacified him; he desisted from the operations, and his good humour as quickly returned."

When the ships entered the main stream of the river and the colour of the water turned from khaki to pewter, the crews were in perfect health. They congratulated themselves on having passed unscathed through the dreaded delta which had proved so fatal to their predecessors. They could not realise that *anopheles gambiae* is not, in fact, a mosquito of the swamps, but prefers the savannah to the forest. So, just as they began to find the country more inviting and the climate more temperate, fever struck. William Allen was one of the first victims and soon the disease was making "fearful progress". Trotter called it "river fever", "because the surgeons report it to be of a nature not treated in any work on the subject."

As before, the majesty of the scenery at the confluence made a grand impression on the newcomers. The broad expanse of waters where the two great rivers met, bounded by high mountains, the friendliness of the villagers on the slopes of Mount Stirling, all welcomed them to the spot where the Model Farm was to be established. According to Trotter, the Nufi people called the place Mount Patteh or Pattee, the Kakenda inhabitants called it Lokosa, which became Lokoja. By a deed of cession, a tract of land sixteen miles long on the west bank was purchased for 700,000 cowries, or £45. Mr Carr, three Europeans and a score of negroes were landed to begin work, while Trotter intended to take the *Albert* up to Rabba and Allen to go up the Benue in the *Wilberforce*, while the *Soudan* returned down river with the sick. Allen protested that neither he nor the crew were in a fit state of health to proceed and suggested that the *Wilberforce* should follow the *Soudan* downstream. Trotter agreed to the change of plan, taking Schön and Crowther on board his ship and transferring all the sick to Allen's, so that with her decks encumbered with hammocks and cots under awnings the *Wilberforce* looked like a hospital ship.

On September 21 she set off downstream, thrashing her way as fast as possible in order to take advantage of the flood water. Within five days she reached the delta, to be engulfed with heat, the "stillness of death broken only by the strokes and echoes of our paddle-wheels and the melancholy song of the leadsmen, which seemed the knell and dirge of our dying comrades." At Fernando Po Bird Allen died and William Allen stretched across to Ascension to restore the health of his men. When he returned, he found the *Albert* there, Trotter being lifted out of his cot to welcome him.

The *Albert* had got as far as Egga in the Nufi country before fever forced her to return with only one seaman left fit for duty. Nothing, wrote Schön at this point, "that I have hitherto seen or felt can be compared with our present condition. Pain of body, distress of mind, sorrow, sobbing and crying, surround us on all sides. The healthy, if so they may be called, are more like walking shadows than men of enterprise. Truly Africa is an unhealthy country! When will her redemption draw nigh? All human skill is baffled – all human means fall short."

He, with Dr MacWilliam and Dr Stanger, the geologist, were the only Europeans still immune. The latter studied a manual of steam navigation in order to work the engines. As Trotter's despatch puts it, "Dr Stanger in the most spirited manner, after consulting Tredgold's work on steam, and getting some little instruction from a convalescent engineer, has undertaken to work the engines himself" – with the surgeon, using Allen's old chart, to navigate the ship. Providentially, when they reached the confluence and the engines broke down once more they met the little *Ethiope*, which Beecroft ("a fine old veteran of the coast") had brought up to their assistance. She took the *Albert* in tow and the two ships managed to reach Fernando Po in safety.

Since Allen had recovered his health on his cruise in the open sea, he wished to take his ship up river once again on what would have been his third voyage up the Niger; but the government, having received Trotter's lugubrious despatch, decided to call off the expedition with orders that they both return home immediately. Lieutenant W. H. Webb was therefore put in command of the *Wilberforce* in order to take off any survivors from the farm. On July 2, 1842, Webb crossed the bar once more. It was the dry season, so that sandbanks and fallen trees almost blocked the stream. From the Obi he heard news of a Fulani attack on the settlement and the mysterious disappearance of Mr Carr, whose fate was never known – though Webb suspected that the Obi knew more about it than he cared to tell. They reached the confluence in a fortnight to find that the rumours were true. There was no sign of Carr and in the manager's absence the workers had begun to quarrel amongst themselves. All the stores, with the negro workers, were taken off and the half-cultivated site was left to revert to nature until, twelve years later, the overgrown fields were revisited on a happier occasion.

When the *Wilberforce* followed the *Albert* back to England it was admitted that the expedition had been a disastrous failure. Buxton's Society for Civilising Africa was wound up and there can be no doubt that his own death was hastened by the shock and by the widespread criticism of his ill-advised attempt to convert Africa. As to the slave trade, the lame conclusion which Trotter and Allen came to in their narrative was that the only means of suppressing it was to exhort other nations to play their part. In their view, the British system of "marine police" was useless. A negro colony under British sovereignty was the only hope for the Niger. Such a colony should be established at the confluence, manned by native troops, with an "African marine to ensure the peaceful intercourse of the nations on the banks of the Niger for the furtherance of legitimate commerce and the enforcement of the treaties already entered into for the suppression of the Slave Trade in the river. A principle feature of this plan is the proposition to establish an African Force, the officers of which should be natives, holding commissions, and the sons of native chiefs should be persuaded to enter the army and navy, with a view to educating them for the service. As it is very clear from all the attempts that have been made, that white men cannot serve in that country without great sacrifice, we ought to use the means which are adapted to the end."

They quote the following figures for the annual ratio of deaths per thousand men serving on foreign stations – Mediterranean 9.3; West Indies 18.1; Coast of Africa 58.4. The mortality on Buxton's expedition amounted to 53 out of a complement of 303, but that number included most of the Europeans: 25 in the *Albert*, 11 in the *Wilberforce*, 13 in the *Soudan*; that is to say, 35% of those who left England.

In view of these figures, the Tory government cannot be blamed for refraining from further humanitarian ventures of the type recommended by Buxton and his friends. The disaster postponed further enterprise on the Niger for ten years. What was worse, it gave impetus to the heterogeneous collection of people who either wished to reduce the Squadron or even to withdraw altogether from West Africa. These included pacifists, who opposed any form of coercion; naval officers, pessimistic about the results of thirty years' effort; crypto-fascists like Carlyle with his "beneficent whip", or Professor Merivale of Oxford who thought that slavery was not such a bad institution after all; above all, the Free Trade Members of Parliament, who complained of the cost and the way slave trading was now equated with smuggling – they should have said piracy.

Throughout the 1840's these opponents to the national effort to suppress the illegal slave trade made their voices heard throughout the land. Four Select Parliamentary Committees examined the question and, having reported at extravagant length, came to contradictory conclusions. The case for suppression would certainly have been lost had not Lord John Russell, as Prime Minister, spoken up in its defence.

Success in ending the Brazilian trade early in the 'fifties by a combination of naval force and diplomatic effort showed what could be done, so that the ultimate consequence of the great debate was to strengthen the Squadron and intensify the political effort. Even so, had not Palmerston made it his "benevolent crotchet" (as Cobden complained) and adopted his usual methods in foreign policy of bullying the weaker offenders, such as the Portuguese, and annexing notorious slave ports, such as Lagos, in 1851, the extinction of the trade would have required another thirty years' effort, even if the North had not won the American Civil War.

Only after these steps had been taken against the traffic in slaves could there be any renewed attempt to encourage legitimate trade up the Niger; and only as a result of closer study of the fever problem on board the ships of the Squadron could the barrier of disease be overcome.

9

The Travels of Dr Barth

Henry Barth, Ph.D., as he called himself for the benefit of English readers of the five thick volumes describing his travels in northern Nigeria and the western Soudan, is the most neglected of the great African explorers. Something has been done recently to justify the words of the President of the Royal Geographical Society at the time of his death: "A more intelligent, indefatigable, trustworthy and resolute traveller than Dr Barth can rarely be found." Lord Rennell of Rodd, who held the same office a hundred years later and who had himself traversed the same part of the Sahara, called him "perhaps the greatest traveller there has ever been in Africa." Between those dates hardly any interest was evinced in Barth's very considerable achievements.

Perhaps it was the Ph.D. which alienated the public, for he had all the virtues and all the failings associated with a doctorate: industry, care, an arid style and the absence not only of a sense of humour but of any sense of the dramatic. As Professor of Geography at the University of Berlin, who wrote at enormous length in both German and English, he was not the type of traveller to engage the attention of a public enthralled by the search for Sir John Franklin, or excited by the narrative of Livingstone's first journey, which was published at the same time as Barth's *Travels and Discoveries in North and Central Africa: being a journal of an expedition undertaken under the auspices of H.M. Government in the years 1849–55*. Livingstone's book sold over 50,000 copies; Barth's scarcely 2,250. Yet the two men met and exchanged signed copies in mutual admiration. Both were solitaries, travelling alone for the most part of their long sojourns in the unknown interior; but whereas Livingstone's transparent humanity and selfless zeal endeared him to the British public, Barth's strictly scientific approach to his task of delineating a new area of the continent in 3,500 pages had little appeal. Nevertheless, this habit of recording observations made over a period of five and a half years on a journey of 10,000 miles has ensured the lasting value of what is still the standard account of the area lying between Timbuktu on the upper Niger and Lake Chad, with the sources of the Niger's greatest tributary, the Benue, far away to the east.

Heinrich Barth was born of strict Lutheran stock at Hamburg in 1821. Schoolfellows tell of his efforts to strengthen a weak constitution by cold baths and physical exercises, as well as his eccentric interest in everything Arabian. He spoke English fluently as a boy and was an accomplished Arabist by the time he went to the university. There he interrupted his studies to travel in Italy, the goal and limit of most young Germans of his generation. When he returned to Berlin to lecture on classical geography, his delivery was so bad and his material so dull that no one attended his classes, so that he was soon off again to travel through the provinces of the old Turkish Empire and the shores of north Africa. At Tunis a Hausa slave said to him: "Please God, you shall go and visit Kano." "These words were constantly ringing in my ears; and though overpowered for a time by the vivid impressions of interesting and picturesque countries, they echoed with renewed intensity as soon as I was restored to the tranquillity of European life."

His opportunity came in 1849. The British government, in which Palmerston was Foreign Secretary, had agreed to proposals of James Richardson, a disciple of Fowell Buxton, to penetrate south of the Sahara in order to gather material for the suppression of the slave trade at its source, and "to raise up degraded Africa to civilised Europe." From those words alone it may be deduced that he was an ardent member of the Anti-Slavery Society. The failure of Buxton's attempt to "civilise" the Niger from the south made the authorities in London (who still made the suppression of the trade their main interest in Africa) prefer an approach from the north, in much the same way as the tragedy of Mungo Park's death resulted in the mission to Bornu a generation earlier.

As the agent of the Anti-Slavery Society, Richardson had already reached Murzuk and Ghat on a fact-finding mission. He had intended to go further south, even to Timbuktu, but ill health compelled him to return. Evidence of his zeal in the cause may be seen in the appeal which he circulated to other missionary societies on his return to London: "If the Christian Churches were to vindicate the honour of their religion, to diffuse its heavenly and beneficent doctrines and to remove from themselves the severe censure of having abandoned Central Africa to the fake Prophet, I believe there is now an opening via Bornu to attempt the establishment of that faith in the heart of Africa."

He then approached the Foreign Office with an ambitious plan to open up "a regular and secure way of communication over the Sahara from the Mediterranean to the banks of the Niger," the first step in which must be the despatch of an official mission to Bornu and Lake Chad, a region which had remained unvisited since the days of Major Denham.

Palmerston agreed, provided that he was accompanied by a scientist who could plot the position of towns in the empire of Bornu, as the insufferable Denham had so signally failed to do. An approach was made to the French, and when that failed, to the Prussian Ambassador in London. The latter passed it on to the great geographers then teaching at Berlin, Von Humboldt and Carl Ritter, who promptly suggested Barth. He was described as thirty-three years of age, a remarkable linguist and one who had travelled widely in

Arab-speaking countries. In fact, Barth was twenty-eight, had spent only half the stated time abroad, and was not a scientist but a geographer. However, provided he paid £200 for the privilege, he was accepted in London, and a younger man, Adolf Overweg, was also taken on at the price of £150. Barth's father objected to these terms, fearing that the expedition would prejudice his son's chances of promotion. The dutiful Heinrich obeyed and tried to withdraw, but the government replied that a contract had been made and that Richardson was waiting to start.

Barth therefore went to London to meet him. In the preface to his book he calls it "a generous act of Lord Palmerston to allow two foreign gentlemen to join it instead of one," but the terms of the contract hardly suggest this, and the way he was kept perpetually short of cash (as his predecessors had been) while in Africa gives some excuse to his later complaint that he was "reduced to a beggar abroad." As usual, the Treasury wanted exploration on the cheap. When it is reckoned that it cost only £1,600 to maintain him for five years (of which he himself paid £200), Barth's expedition must have been the cheapest on record.

He knew, however, that he could depend on the moral, if not the financial, support of the British Consul at Tripoli. This was "my kind friend, Mr Frederick Warrington", the son of Colonel Hanmer Warrington, who had befriended Clapperton, Laing and others so long ago. Barth had met the Colonel, who died in 1847, on his previous travels, when "he seems to have had some presentiment of my capabilities as an African explorer, and even promised me his full assistance if I should penetrate into the interior. Besides this, my admiration of the wide extension of the British over the globe, their influence, their language, and their government, was such that I felt a strong inclination to become an honourable means of carrying out their philanthropic view for the progressive civilisation of the neglected races of

Central Africa. Under these circumstances, I undertook cheerfully to accompany Mr Richardson, on the sole condition, however, that the exploration of Central Africa should be made the principal object of the mission, instead of a secondary one, as had been originally contemplated."

In making this stipulation Barth again failed to carry his point. Richardson was appointed the official leader, partly because of his experience, brief as it was, but chiefly because he represented the Evangelical interest and was the agent to explore the possibilities of making the anti-slavery and commercial treaties which were the official excuse for the expedition. Having led the "two scientific gentlemen" across the desert, they were to part company in the region of Lake Chad, from which point the Germans were at liberty to go where they wanted – to push on eastwards to the Nile, south-eastwards towards Mombasa, or west to Timbuktu. Barth sensibly chose the latter route, partly because it was the only feasible one, partly because after the death of his companions he was left without financial resources.

They were an ill-assorted group of travellers. Richardson was a zealous missionary with no interest in exploration. To judge from his journal, he was a dull fellow, an indifferent manager and chiefly interested in writing an account of his adventures for the benefit of his missionary friends. Barth is reticent about their relations, but the consuls at Tunis, Tripoli and Murzuk were more outspoken in their despatches. The former reported that "the Germans and our Englishman do not appear to pull very well together, and there seems to be a degree of jealousy between them. It strikes me also that the Germans are scientific men and Mr Richardson the bookmaker only." Consul Warrington helped them to buy camels, lent them a tent, entertained them generously at Tripoli, and then wrote: "I am disgusted with the ingratitude of Richardson. I fear that his wretched mismanagement will lower the reputation enjoyed by the English nation in

Central Africa." The consul at Murzuk, the last town to be visited before crossing the Sahara, said much the same thing: "He is too confident in himself and listens little to advice. May God protect them!"

Barth is more forthcoming and more critical about Adolf Overweg, an enthusiastic young man who treated the whole thing as a great adventure rather than a serious scientific enterprise. Overweg kept no notes; he lacked method; after his death it was impossible to trust or even understand the observations he was supposed to have made for cartographical purposes. "He was deficient in that general Knowledge of natural science which is required for comprehending all the various phenomena occurring on the journey into unknown regions. Having never before risked his life on a dangerous expedition, he never for a moment doubted that it might not be his good fortune to return home in safety." Certainly his methods of doctoring the natives argue a cheerful disregard for science. "His practice was rather of a remarkable kind," says Barth benevolently; "for he used generally to treat his patients, not according to the character of their sickness, but according to the days of the week on which they came. Thus he had one day of calomel, another of Dover's powders, one of Epsom salts, one of magnesia, one of tartar emetic."

The three men met briefly in London. Richardson declared that he must wait in Paris for further despatches; the two Germans decided to go on ahead, landing at Tunis on December 15, 1849. They spent the waiting interval wandering in the neighbouring mountains. A few camels were bought and two servants engaged. One, Mohammed el Gatroni, remained with Barth throughout his stay in Africa; the other was soon sent home when he proved to be an impudent and dissolute rascal. Later on Barth bought and liberated two negro boys, whom he brought back to Europe with him. One, Abegga, returned to settle at Lokoja, of which he became chief, while his son became a Bornu chief who died only a few years ago. The other, a remarkably intelligent lad, called Durogu, became the source of a quarrel with the Rev. Schön, whom we met in the last chapter.

At last, in March, 1850, Richardson arrived at Tripoli, where Warrington had been entertaining his companions: "Mr Frederick Warrington is perhaps the most amiable possible specimen of an Arabianised European. To this gentleman, whose zeal in the objects of the expedition was beyond all praise, I must be allowed to pay my tribute as a friend," wrote the grateful Barth. He was even more grateful when Warrington said he would accompany them on the first stage of their journey to Murzuk, thus easing the meeting with Richardson, whose conduct up to that point had not reassured them.

Before they crossed the sea of pebbles known as the Hamada el Homra, or "fearful burning plain", Warrington turned back. The progress of their caravan was so slow, now that they were in the desert, that Barth had plenty of opportunity to sketch and explore on his own account. On one of these occasions he went too far, got lost among the mountains of sand and gave himself up for lost. For the most part, the two Germans kept together, finding Richardson deaf, slow and uncommunicative, but as they entered the mountains of Air, the stronghold of the Tuareg, the continuous harassment and blackmail to which they were subjected drew them together. Robbery turned to threats of murder, which their Arab companions took so seriously that they gave the Christians up for lost and made no attempt to protect them.

"Our people were so firmly convinced that, as we stoutly refused to change our religion, though only for a day or two, we should immediately suffer death, that our servant Mohammed, as well as Mukai, requested us most urgently to testify, in writing, that they were innocent of our blood. . . .

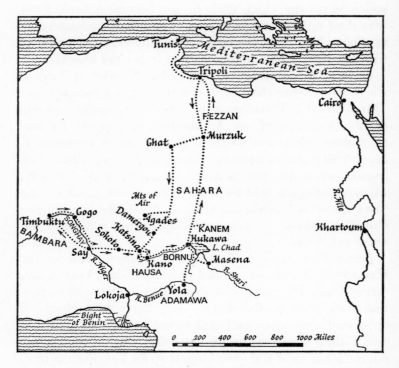

We were sitting silently in our tent, with the inspiring consciousness of going to our fate in a manner worthy alike of our religion and of the nation in whose name we were travelling among these barbarous tribes, when Mr Richardson interrupted the silence which prevailed with the words: 'Let us talk a little. We must die; what is the use of sitting so mute?' For some minutes death really seemed to hover over our heads; but the awful moment passed by. We had been discussing Mr Richardson's propositions for an attempted escape with our lives, when, as a forerunner of the official messenger, the benevolent and kind-hearted Sliman rushed into our tent and with the most sincere sympathy stammered out the few words, 'You are not to die'."

Under such circumstances it says much for Barth's courage that he resolved to visit by himself the city of Agades, which he considered rivalled Timbuktu in importance, though it was virtually unknown in Europe. When he rejoined his companions, "I felt as if I had enjoyed a glimpse of a totally different world, a new region of life." Now he could join in the enthusiastic cry which went up from the caravan, "No rest before Kano!"

When they emerged from the wastes of the Sahara into the savannah country, the home of the giraffe and the antelope, it was agreed that the three white men should part company, each going his own way to Kukawa (or Kouka, as Barth spells it in his letters), the capital of the Bornu empire on the shores of Lake Chad, where they would meet on April 1. Barth was determined to reach Kano on his own account, nor was he sorry to bid farewell to Richardson at Damergou on January 10, 1851. Yet it was with "a sinister feeling" that he did so. Richardson was obviously suffering from the heat, in spite of his habit of sheltering under his umbrella throughout the march. Barth very much doubted whether he had the health or the heart to sustain a long journey on his own. As for himself, "I now went on alone, but felt not at all depressed by solitude, as I had been accustomed from my youth to wander about by myself among strange people."

It was due to his early training in living among Arabs as equals that he was now enabled to strike up friendships wherever he went. He had very little money and few presents to repay hospitality. Indeed, by the end of his journey he was almost penniless. This constant shortage of cash made him an object of scorn among the rulers of Negroland (as he calls this part of Central Africa). It was only his tact and obvious sincerity that allowed him to continue on friendly terms with his servants and his companions in the caravan. Thus, when the governor of Katsina, the first important town which he reached, forbade him to join the caravan to Kano, his friends loyally explained his humiliating poverty by explaining how he had been robbed en route.

He reached Kano, "the celebrated emporium of Central Negroland", in the best of spirits. Riding a horse was a welcome change after riding a camel, and the Hausa country through which he passed was so pleasant and fertile, its inhabitants so cheerful and industrious that a new world seemed to open before him. As they approached the city, their guide expatiated on its size and riches, the multitudes which thronged its market, the beauty of its women, until "at times my fiery Tunisian mulatto shouted out from mere anticipation of the pleasures which awaited him."

Nor were they disappointed. A massive circle of walls enclosed an enormous area of ground, only a third of which was inhabited. Even the stench of the swamp in the middle of the town which had been so offensive to Clapperton is hardly mentioned in Barth's ecstatic description of the goal of his travels, which had taken him a year to reach. Even his first attack of fever and his continuing poverty did not diminish his admiration of what seemed to be the real capital of Negroland. Timbuktu might be better known, but it was nothing to this place in economic or geographical importance, lying as it did on the junction of trade routes north and south, east and west. His "mediators" once more explained to the governor why this foreigner was so short of money, so that his standing as a visitor was properly enhanced. Allowed to wander at will through this huge, sprawling town, he was impressed by the skill of its inhabitants and the extent of its manufactures and trade in cloth and leather goods, salt and corn, even the export of 5,000 slaves a year. But it was Kano's geographical location which inspired the most accurate of his predictions, that "it will certainly at some future date become important even for the commercial world of Europe."

What depressed him was the failure of the English to exploit the advantages of their discoveries on the Niger.

"I must here speak about a point of very great importance for the English, both as regards their honour and their commercial activity. The final opening of the lower course of the Kwara [Niger] has been one of the most glorious achievements of English discovery, bought with the lives of so many enterprising men. But it seems that the English are more apt to perform a great deed than to follow up the consequences. After they have opened this noble river to the knowledge of Europe, frightened by the sacrifice of a few lives, instead of using it themselves for the benefit of the natives of the interior, they have allowed it to fall into the hands of the American slave-dealers, who have opened a regular annual slave trade with these very regions, while the English seem not to have even the slightest idea of such a traffic going on. Thus American produce, brought in large quantities to the market of Nupe, have begun to inundate Central Africa, to the great damage of the commerce and the most unqualified scandal of the Arabs, who think the English, if they would, could easily prevent it. For this is not a legitimate commerce; it is nothing but slave-traffic on a large scale, the Americans taking nothing in return for their merchandise and their dollars but slaves, besides a small quantity of natron [carbonate of soda]. On this painful subject I have written repeatedly to H.M. Government, and I have spoken energetically about it to Lord Palmerston since my return. I principally regret in this respect the death of Mr Richardson, who, in his eloquent language, would have dealt worthily with this question. But even from his unfinished journals it is clear that during his stay in the country before he was doomed to succumb, he became well aware of what was going on."

As he continued his journey eastward, Barth entered the empire of Bornu, of which Kukawa (Denham's Kuka) was the capital. Before reaching it, he heard of the death of Richardson from some unspecified disease and when he visited his grave he made this comment: "My way of looking at things was not quite the same as that of my late companion, and we therefore had little differences, but I esteemed him highly for the deep sympathy which he felt for the sufferings of the native Africans, and deeply lamented his death."

When he reached the town on April 2 he was allowed to take possession of Richardson's papers which, with his journal, he sent back to England. The vizir had been warned of his arrival, so that he was given good quarters and even lent some money to pay his faithful servants, pending the arrival of fresh supplies from Tripoli. He thoroughly enjoyed his stay there, though when his friend Overweg arrived he looked "greatly fatigued and much worse than when I left him four months ago. Perhaps the news of our companion's death made him uneasy about his own illness." Poor Overweg – it was not long before he, too, succumbed.

Barth's description of the country and history of Bornu is exceedingly long and detailed, including a chronology of its rulers going back to before the days of the Prophet. His only disappointment was Lake Chad, which appeared at that season to be nothing but a swampy plain. It was impossible to survey its shores because these did not exist: in the rainy season neighbouring villages were flooded; in the summer the waters retreated to such an extent that only a small portion was navigable.

In a despatch to the Foreign Secretary dated May 20, 1851, he accurately predicts the next stage of his travels and gives the reasons for them, formed after consultation with knowledgeable Arabs in the town:

"I have the honour to inform your Lordship that I am to start for Adamawa, as it is called by the Fellatah [Fulani], a very extensive country whose capital, Yola, is distant from here fifteen days SSW, situated on a very considerable river called Faro, which, joining another river not less considerable, and likewise navigable, called Benuwe, falls into the Kwara or Niger at a place between Kakanda and Adda [i.e. Lokoja], no more than a few days distant from the mouth of the celebrated river. . . . For my part, I can at present certify with the greatest confidence that there is no connection between these two rivers – the Chadda, which is identical with the Benuwe, and the Shary, the principal tributary of Lake Tsad. Nevertheless, the Faro as well as the Benuwe seem to have their sources to the East of Kukawa; and the river formed by these two branches, being navigable for large boats into the very heart of Adamawa, there will be a great facility for Europeans to enter that country after it has been sufficiently explored. By and by, I am sure, a southern road will be opened into the heart of Central Africa, but the time has not yet come."

The discovery of the upper waters of the Benue, and the fact that it had no direct connection with Lake Chad, as everyone had supposed, was Barth's most important geographical discovery. After striking south, he crossed the great river on June 18 on his way to Yola:

"The principal river, the Benuwe, flowed here from east to west in a broad majestic course, through entirely open country, . . . It was followed in thought till it joined the great western river, the Kwara or Niger; and, conjointly with it, ran towards the great ocean. . . . I looked long and silently upon the stream; it was one of the happiest moments of my life; although for some time uncertain as to the identity of the river of Adamawa with that laid down in its lower course by Messrs W. Allen, Laird and Oldfield, I had long made up my mind on this point, thanks to clear information received from my friend Ahmed bel Mejab. I had now with my own eyes clearly established the direction and nature of this mighty river; and to an unprejudiced mind there could no longer be any doubt that this river joins the majestic watercourse explored by the gentlemen just mentioned. Hence I cherish the well-founded conviction that along this natural highway European influence and commerce will penetrate into the very heart of the continent, and abolish slavery, or rather those infamous slave-hunts and religious wars, destroying the natural germs of human happiness and spreading devastation and desolation all around."

Barth crossed the Benue only a short distance above the point reached by Baikie two years later, after the latter (as will be seen) had been told to look for him in this part of Africa. By that date, Barth was in fact in Timbuktu. Had he received permission from the ruler of Yola to proceed down the river, as he intended, he would have met the expedition coming up from the south, but he was refused on the grounds that the province was only the fief of the Sultan of Sokoto and nothing could be done without the latter's permission. As Barth was now so weak with fever that he could hardly keep his seat on a horse, he was not altogether sorry to be forced to return to Kukawa.

There he found letters from England, but no cash. However, the companionship of Overweg helped him to recover his health, and the two men spent the rest of the year on extensive and strenuous expeditions, much as Denham and Clapperton had done. But in 1852 Overweg's health declined, so that by the autumn he was a dying man. Barth was at his deathbed in September at one of the villages on the shores of Lake Chad.

It was chiefly the loss of his young companion which finally decided him to strike west in search of new lands and new peoples. While at Kukawa he had begun an extensive correspondence with an academic geographer, Desborough Cooley, whose book, *Negroland of the Arabs*, he admired, although it was entirely based on printed material. These letters (hitherto unpublished) are chiefly notes about the countries and the peoples he encountered, but they also contain some valuable personal details. Their syntax betrays Barth's teutonic origin and their obvious depth of feeling show his longing for contact with a fellow Arabist who was perhaps the only man who knew anything about the regions in which he was travelling.

Replying to a letter from Cooley in which he was warned against "rushing blindfold in the hope of groping your way 2,000 miles through barbarous nations," either in the direction of Mombasa or Timbuktu, Barth wrote on July 26, 1852 that he had decided to turn west. He begged Cooley "not to take me for a child. It has never been my intention to rush blindfold into any situation whatever. It is true, to reach the coast of the Indian Ocean and to determine the nature of the equatorial regions of Central Africa and if possible to make out the country from whence the Nile does take its origin, has been from the beginning my favourite idea. But it has always been an idea, never my intention. My intention has been, after having visited all the countries round our headquarters to try to penetrate as far as possible from these points to extend our researches as (far as) possible. From the beginning, I have kept open the choice between an Easterly or a South-Easterly road, according to experience and circumstances, and it was in the beginning of last year that in a letter sent home I expressed my intention, if experience should be against an E or SE road, to turn my face Westwards."

The day after Overweg's death he describes how he is "now lonely and companionless in these regions, where nobody does understand my doings, the Director of my own expedition, but nevertheless in good health and best spirits, as far as circumstances will allow, and shall not give up the least point. I am not a man who is afraid of death in such a cause, but I shall be more prudent and it will, please God, I trust to give me success and after that a safe return home, redeemed by the sacrifice of two lives out of three. . . . I tell you that I have full confidence in my safe return and in my being able to lay the proceedings of this expedition in an elaborated form before the public. . . ."

In November he set out for Kano and Katsina, where he was lucky enough to take delivery of 1,000 dollars sent from Tripoli. As far as the authorities were concerned, for the next two years he was lost in the interior and presumed dead like the others. In fact, by the beginning of 1853 he had recovered his spirits and was being royally entertained by the Sultan of Sokoto. He was shown Clapperton's house and apologies were made for the way the late Sultan had neglected him, the reason given being that he was engaged in a war. His chief discovery in this part of the world was at Gando (Gwendu), where he found a rare copy of the chronicle called Turikh-es-Soudan, which only he realised was the basis of almost all that is known about the early history of western Africa.

Continuing west, he reached the Niger at Say, where there was a ford across "the great river of western Africa which has aroused so much curiosity in Europe, and the upper part of the eastern part of which [i.e. the Benue] I had myself discovered." This was on June 23. "The great river, whose name, under whatever form it may appear, whether Dhiuliba [Joliba], Mayo, Eghirrev, Isa, Kwara [Quorra] or Baki-n-ruwa, means nothing but 'the river', and which therefore may well continue to be called the Niger, was gliding along, in a NNE and SSW direction, with a moderate current of about three miles an hour."

From this point he cut across the great bend of the river in a north-westerly direction, in order to reach Timbuktu by the shortest overland route. His resources and his health were at a low ebb. He had been alone for a year, and he was so ill when he arrived at his destination on the anniversary of Overweg's death that he feared that he himself would suffer the same fate. Calling himself Abdul Karim ("the merciful one") or styling himself "the messenger of the Sultan of Stanbul", and, as always, clothed as an Arab, with his skin stained with indigo, he claimed the protection of Sheikh El Bakay, the leader of a desert tribe which was in dispute with a fanatical faction of the Fulani, the overlords of the city. The father of one of the latter had been responsible for the murder of Major Laing in 1826. Barth identified him as Sheikh Ahmed Dakidi el Habib, who was still alive, as he told Cooley. Somehow the man was convinced that Barth was Laing's son and that it was his duty to assassinate him. When, however, the man died suddenly the feeling in the town veered in favour of the stranger who claimed its hospitality.

In view of the tense political situation within the city, Barth could not have arrived at a worse moment. His situation improved after the arrival of El Bakay on the outskirts of the town, but for the next eight months he was a pawn in a complicated war game between the two parties. In this part of his narrative his pedestrian style rises above the usual humdrum description of towns and peoples to a stirring story of intrigue and counter-intrigue, plots and counter-plots, sudden imprisonments and equally sudden releases, while armed bands prowled around the city and excited threats passed between supporters and enemies within its walls. While endless consultations about what was to be done with him continued over his head, all he could do was to fortify himself with cups of tea and keep his shotgun well oiled.

Gradually El Bakay's supporters gained the upper hand, though Barth was not permitted to depart because (as one of them told him) it was customary to keep guests at Timbuktu for at least a year. Nor did the news of French attacks on affiliated tribes in Algeria make the situation of a white man easier.

There were compensations for his long stay. The Sheikh was a charming and intelligent man, who insisted on Barth accompanying him on his expeditions. Among his entourage there were many cultivated Arabs, or *mullams*, with whom Barth had long and interesting conversations, even though he was a *kafir* or unbeliever. One man drew out of his pocket a volume of Hippocrates in order to identify a plant mentioned in it. Clapperton had given the book to Sultan Bello long ago and, as Barth comments, "I may assert with full confidence that these few books taken by the gallant captain into Central Africa have had a greater effect in reconciling the men in authority in Africa to the character of Europeans than the most costly presents ever made to them."

They even had friendly religious arguments, with Barth defending Christianity by very curious arguments:

"Sidi Mohammed had made a serious attack upon my religion, and called me always a Kafir. But I told him that I was a real Moslem, the pure Islam, the true worship of the one God, dating from the time of Adam, and not from the time of Mohammed; and that thus, while adhering to the principle of unity, and the most spiritual and sublime nature of the Divine Being, I was a Moslem, professing the real Islam, although not adopting the worldly statutes of Mohammed, who only followed the principles established long before his time. I likewise added that even they themselves regarded Plato and Aristotle as Moslemin, and that thus I myself was to be regarded as a Moslem, in a much stricter sense than the two pagan philosophers."

Despatches from England somehow reached him at Timbuktu, informing him that another German scientist, Dr Vogel, had been sent to find him; but nothing was said about plans for Dr Baikie's expedition up the Niger, of which Barth had no official confirmation until after his return home; yet one of Baikie's instructions was to find him when he was still supposed to be on the upper Benue.

All this made Barth the more anxious to depart after such
a long and enforced stay. He remembered what happened to
Laing. He confirmed what Caillié had written about the
place in 1828, thus restoring confidence in a romantic
narrative on which some doubt had been cast in both
England and France. He was entirely dependent on the
charity and protection of El Bakay, being well aware that the
Sheikh's opponents might gain the upper hand at any
moment, and he was constantly informed of their intention
to kill him as an infidel if they succeeded. Three months
"after my happy arrival at this ill-famed place", he told
Cooley on November 27, 1853, he was patiently awaiting
his departure. On March 13, 1854, he was still there among
his "fanatic and unjust" enemies. "It seems not quite
impossible after all that I shall finally leave this town, of
which I am greatly tired, in a very few days. May the merciful God grant me a safe return; my way is a long and difficult
one. I shall drink a glass of water from the Niger upon your
health in Gogo."

Even at his departure he was made aware just how pre-
carious his situation was:

"In the meantime the Tawarek [Tuareg] whom we had
with us beat their shields in their usual furious manner, and
raised the war cry; the night was very dark, and I at length
fired a shot which informed my friends of our whereabouts.
We found the Sheikh close to the town with a large host of
people, Tawarek as well as Arabs, Songhay and even Fullan.
The spectacle formed by this multifarious host, thronging
among the sandhills in the pale moonlight, was highly
interesting, and would have been the more so to me if I
could have been a tranquil observer of the scene; but as I
was the chief cause of this disturbance, several of my friends
begged me to beware of treachery. The Sheikh himself
despatched his most trustworthy servant to inform me that I
had better keep in the midst of the Tawarek, whom he

himself thought much more trustworthy than the Arabs. The Keluli forthwith formed a square round me, but at the same time made a joke of it, trying an experiment as to the warlike disposition of my horse by pushing against me, till I spurred my horse and drove them to their former position. Excited by this animated scene, my noble charger, to the great amusement of this turbulent host, began to neigh from sheer delight."

When he was at last permitted to go on his way in the middle of May the Sheikh accompanied him along the banks of the Niger as far as Gogo (or Geo), an important town on the extreme bend of the river which had once been the capital of the Songhay empire but was now in ruins.

"During our stay in this place I had laid down the course of the river between Timbuktu and Gogo on a tolerably large scale, written a despatch to the government, and several letters to members of the Royal Geographical Society and other private friends, and, having sealed the parcel, I delivered it to the Sheikh in order that he might forward it without delay upon his return to Timbuktu. I am sorry, however, that this parcel only arrived a few months ago, having been laid up in Ghadames for more than two years."

In fact, his last letter to Cooley is dated Gogo, June 24, 1854, but superscribed "By Accident, London, July 8, 1856."

Before bidding farewell to his escort he was asked, in order to mark the occasion, to don European dress. It is rather extraordinary that all he had with him at this stage of his journey was a black dress suit with tails, which the Arabs rightly thought "highly absurd. But having never before seen fine black cloth, they were surprised at its appearance and at a distance the people mistook it for a coat of mail, as most of them had been accustomed to see only red cloth."

The parting from Sheikh El Bakay on July 9 was a sad occasion.

"He was the person who, among all the people I had come

in contact in the course of my long journey, I had esteemed the most highly, and whom, in all but his dilatory habits and phlegmatic indifference, I had found a most excellent and trustworthy man."

So he continued on his way by himself, following the course of the river southward as far as Say. From there he wished to go on to Yauri, so that he could describe the whole bend of the river from the point where Park had described it above Timbuktu to the point reached by Lander from the south; but he was told that this was impossible. A rebellion had broken out further down river and he himself was once more without resources. It was important to reach Sokoto before the rains broke, where among the Hausa people he knew that he would find a friendly reception.

At Sokoto he first heard of Vogel's arrival at Kukawa. He expresses unreasonable anger that he had not been told of this, but as he was given up for dead there was no means of getting in touch with him; nor, it must be confessed, had Vogel made much attempt to do so. Similarly, at Kano he heard rumours of a steamboat on the lower Niger, but he did not know for certain about Baikie's expedition until after his return home.

The actual meeting between Barth and Vogel reminds one of that between Stanley and Livingstone, though in Barth's undramatic style it is not so memorable. The date was December 1 and Barth was on the road nearing Kukawa "when I saw advancing towards me a person of strange aspect – a young man of very fair complexion, dressed in a tobe [shirt] like the one I wore myself, and with a white turban wound thickly round his head. He was accompanied by two or three blacks, likewise on horseback. One of them I recognised as my servant Madi, whom, when on setting out from Kukawa, I had left in the house as a guardian. As soon as he saw me he told the young man that I was Abdul Kerim, in consequence of which Mr Vogel (for he it was) rushed forward, and, taken by surprise as both of us were, we gave each other a hearty reception from horseback. As for myself, I had not the remotest idea of meeting him; and he, on his part, had only a short time before received the intelligence of my safe return from the west. Not having the slightest notion that I was alive, and judging from its Arab address that the letter which I forwarded to him from Kano was a letter from an Arab, he had put it by without opening it, waiting till he might meet with a person who should be able to read it. In the midst of this inhospitable forest, we dismounted and sat down together on the ground; and, my camels having arrived, I took out my small bag of provisions and had some coffee boiled, so that we were quite at home."

Vogel's casual behaviour did not endear him to a man of Barth's precise temperament and when he reached Kukawa to find all supplies and correspondence addressed to this inexperienced young man, his anger with the authorities at home broke out afresh:

"All the mismanagement in consequence of the false news of my death greatly enhanced the unpleasant nature of my situation; for, instead of leaving the country under honourable circumstances, I was considered as almost disgraced by those who had sent me out, the command having been taken from me and given to another. There is no doubt that such an opinion delayed my departure considerably."

May 19, 1855 was thus the date on which he started the return journey across the desert, going due north to Murzuk and Tripoli, "and I turned my back with great satisfaction upon those countries where I had spent five full years in incessant toil and exercise." At Tripoli he was at least refreshed with a bottle of wine from Warrington's cellar, something which he had been looking forward to for a very long time. A passage back to London was arranged, so that he arrived back in England in September, the exact date being doubtful.

His return passed almost unnoticed by a public engrossed in the later stages of the Crimean War and the discoveries made in east Africa. His own discoveries were not of the dramatic type, like that of a snow-capped mountain (Mt Kilimanjaro) on the equator, recently seen by two missionaries, Rebmann and Krapf; still less Livingstone's discovery of the Victoria Falls, or the travels of Burton and Speke in search of the source of the Nile, which were soon to start. Nevertheless, the Foreign Office granted him a pension of £500 for the next five years and advanced £2,000 towards the expense of printing his narrative, the first three volumes of which appeared in 1857, the remainder in 1858.

These 3,500 pages never became popular with the general public, though geographers immediately acclaimed the high standard of the maps and the beauty of the lithographs drawn after his sketches. In modern times the accuracy of his descriptions of a part of Africa which is still mysterious have been much admired. He was not content to describe the scenery of the countries through which he passed, but widened his investigations into the character of the peoples which inhabited them, their economy, their politics and history, so that his work has been aptly described as an exploration in time as well as space. As he wrote in his preface, "We here trace a historical thread which guides us through the labyrinth of tribes and overthrown kingdoms." And time has justified his concluding sentence:

"I have the satisfaction to feel that I have opened to the view of the scientific public of Europe a most extensive tract of the secluded African world, and not only made it tolerably known, but rendered the opening of a regular intercourse between Europeans and these regions possible."

The English press may have been grudging in its praise for this indefatigable German, but his reception in Prussia was more gratifying: he was even compared with Herodotus. During the remaining years of his life the rumblings of the

coming Anglo-German rivalry in the Scramble for Africa
were distinctly heard. Not that he himself – at least at first –
was dissatisfied with "the handsome remuneration which Her
Majesty's Government has determined to grant me," but,
like all solitaries, he was a prickly sort of person in his
relations with officialdom, so that his resentment at the
eclipse of his achievements by the explorers of the Nile
increased as the years went by.

The trouble started before his return when his friend and
publisher, August Petermann, printed a pamphlet accusing
the Royal Geographical Society of offensive and inaccurate
remarks about his expedition; for example, that the Society
had not been properly informed, a task which Petermann
tried to remedy that same year with an enormous portfolio
adorned with portraits and an excellent map of the first part
of Barth's journey. Petermann was convinced that there was
in England "an unworthy antipathy against Germans
generally." It is true that the Secretary of the Society, which
regarded itself as the repository of all things African, had
taken umbrage at the failure of the Foreign Office to keep it
properly informed, but most of Barth's despatches had been
read at its meetings. After his return, he himself increased the
tension by speaking of "a few mean-minded individuals
seeking to exploit national enmity under the guise of scholarly
questions, (who) had given vent to their feelings in contemptible utterances against the leadership of an English
expedition by a German." None the less, he was glad to
receive the Gold Medal of the Society, as well as those of the
geographical societies of Paris and Hamburg.

His relations with the British government cooled off
because of his very reasonable grievance that, having been
promised the Order of the Bath (an honour accorded to no
other African explorer), it was not actually conferred for
several years, on account of what he called "a clique of
jealous officials." He was annoyed at not being consulted

over Baikie's second expedition, and even more by the failure of the government to follow up the promises which he had made to El Bakay to open trade negotiations with Timbuktu. Both during his travels and after his return, he was convinced that it was the fault of officialdom that he was perpetually short of money.

Distinguished English friends prevented such grievances from assuming too serious a tone and for a time he even lived in London. He was on good terms with Admiral Smyth, one of the founders of the Royal Geographical Society, Sir Roderick Murchison, who awarded him the Gold Medal, Dr Baikie, when on leave from the Niger, and Sir Richard Burton, another solitary and difficult man. As we have seen, he also met and liked Livingstone on one of the latter's rare visits to this country.

Another body which annoyed him was the Anti-Slavery Society, who criticised him for joining in slave hunts (in which he had no choice), and for bringing back two liberated slaves as his servants. He was so hurt by the latter charge that he arranged for their transport back to Africa, but at Southampton they were taken off the ship by the egregious Rev. Schön, who employed Durogu as his assistant in compiling a dictionary of the Hausa language. Barth had his revenge by attacking the book as unreliable when it was published.

Life in Berlin was not much happier. He quarrelled with Petermann over the failure to send an expedition to see what had become of Vogel. He became President of the Geographical Society, but his old University ignored him until, two years before his death, the Minister of Culture intervened to make him Professor-Extraordinary, which allowed him time and opportunity to travel in southern Europe again and to complete his valuable African vocabularies.

Henry Barth died on November 26, 1865, aged only forty-four. The event elicited a worthy tribute from Murchison to his "indomitable perseverence and skilful researches." Petermann spoke of his "noble character and sterling heart" hidden under a rough exterior. His brother-in-law supports this by describing how in his last years he cut himself off from society:

"His behaviour had taken on the serious, dignified, reserved, proud and almost arrogant quality of the Arab sons of the desert, with whom he had lived so long."

10

Dr Baikie's Settlement

Although the failure of Buxton's expedition up the Niger inclined the government to prefer exploration from the north, the pressure from Exeter Hall for the suppression of the slave trade and the promotion of "legitimate trade" in the lower Niger continued. Charles Dickens was one of those who did not share this Evangelical zeal. In the fourth chapter of *Bleak House* Mrs Jellyby is introduced as a plump little lady "with handsome eyes, though they had a curious habit of seeming to look a long way off. She was a lady of remarkable strength of character, who had devoted herself to an extensive variety of public subjects and especially to the subject of Africa with a view to the cultivation of the coffee berry, and a happy settlement of our superabundant population in Borrioboola-Gha on the left bank of the Niger."

The immediate result of the support of the Evangelical crusade by politicians of the stature of Russell and Palmerston was an improvement in the strength and the tactics of the West African Squadron. More important was the decided improvement in its health, which was due largely to the naval surgeon, Alexander Bryson. In 1847 he presented to the Admiralty a *Report on the Climate and Principal Diseases of the African Station*, in which he was able to announce that the annual mortality rate had been halved. If certain simple precautions were more rigorously observed, such as never sleeping on shore, or reducing boat work up the creeks to a minimum, the chance of infection would be much diminished. Close blockade of the slaving ports was too dangerous, because "no vessel can remain more than a week or two at anchor with safety to the health of the crew," and Fernando Po should be avoided, because "there is not perhaps any spot in the world more detrimental to health." Above all, there should be a far more regular issue of quinine in wine.

Bryson blamed the medical schools at home for neglecting this mode of treatment in favour of the traditional blood-letting and purgatives. With some asperity, he indicated that his fellow naval surgeons knew more about conditions in the tropics than academics in London or Edinburgh. "Cinchona bark and the sulphate of quinine are both extremely useful agents for the prevention of fever; and although it would appear that their power has been considerably underrated, and their administration is apprehended but indifferently understood, still the numerous instances on record in which they have been successfully employed leave no doubt that their more general use upon the station is most urgently required. . . . It is firmly believed that although neither bark nor quinine has the power of preventing the germs of fever from lodging in the system, nevertheless they most decidedly have the power of preventing their development in pyrexial action." When his colleague, Dr Baikie, was sent out on the third Niger expedition in 1854 he attributed its success to Bryson's advice, but it was his own practice which provided the empirical, if not exactly clinical, proof of the efficiency of quinine as a prophylactic. It was Baikie's example more than anything else which provided the long-sought key to African exploration.

By that date another striking improvement in the tactics of suppression had been taken. Disappointed by the failure of African chiefs to adhere to the anti-slavery treaties negotiated with them, the government decided to seize, if not actually annex, the chief places used for the export of slaves. The inspiration for this bold step came from Beecroft, who, after many years of experience in trade and influence in the affairs of the Delta, was appointed Consul of the Bight of Benin and Biafra in 1849, the responsibility of this post extending far beyond that of his predecessor at Fernando Po since it now included Lagos and Dahomey. In Palmerston he found a powerful ally in his determination to alter the direction of British policy from one of non-intervention to one of belligerent action which inevitably led to annexation. None the less, on his appointment the Government specifically disclaimed any "intention to seek to gain possession, either by purchase or otherwise, of any portion of the African continent in those parts." There were now fourteen steam vessels in the Squadron and Beecroft had long been aware of their importance in African affairs, so now he thought there was at least an opportunity of adopting a more militant policy in order to enforce the treaties which he and others had so patiently negotiated.

The first attempt was a failure. Beecroft had been disgusted by the extent of the trade through Whydah, Lagos and Badagry (the miserable place from which the Lander brothers set out). In the summer of 1851 he himself led an abortive attack on Lagos. It was driven off with some loss, but later in the year the ships of the Squadron appeared in greater force to capture the place, though it was not officially annexed for another ten years. This was the first step in establishing a colony on this part of the coast and it was Baikie's companion, Sir John Glover, who became its first Governor.

The effect of the capture of the town and its lagoon was immediate. There was such a rapid expansion in the palm oil trade that Macgregor Laird was encouraged to form the African Steamship Company to cope with it. His efforts to compel the government into taking more interest in the interior were now intensified, so that plans were prepared for a third official expedition up the Niger. Before his death in 1861 he had succeeded in his lifelong aim of forcing the government to support and protect a steamship route up the lower part of the river.

News of Barth's discovery of the upper part of the Benue triggered off the decision to send another expedition. Barth indeed first suggested it to the Prussian Ambassador in London, who passed it on to the Foreign Office. It was to be led by Beecroft on account of his experience. His instructions (which Baikie, as senior medical officer, carried out to him) included an exploration of the river Chadda (i.e. Benue), where an attempt was to be made to make contact with "the excellent traveller" Dr Barth, last heard of in the empire of Bornu. As we have seen, by the time the expedition reached the Benue, Barth was on his way to Timbuktu.

When the decision to send an expedition was announced, Sir Roderick Murchison, then Superintendent of Haslar Hospital, advised one of his junior naval surgeons to volunteer. This was William Balfour Baikie, born in the Orkneys in 1825 and educated at Edinburgh. Like many poor Scottish doctors before him, he joined the Navy as a surgeon-naturalist. He was posted to Haslar, where he impressed Murchison as a potential explorer, combining as he did the training of a doctor with that of a field botanist.

The vessel built by Macgregor Laird for this third expedition, under contract with the Admiralty, was a 260-ton steamer named the *Pleiad*, armed with one 12-pounder pivot gun and four small swivels. The command was entrusted to Beecroft, but when he was on his way out to join the *Pleiad*, Baikie heard of Beecroft's death and realised with a shock that this left him as senior officer of the expedition, so that when he joined the ship he must assume executive command. It was a daunting responsibility for a young surgeon who had never been trained for such duties. That he shouldered such responsibility (albeit unwillingly), and that subsequent events proved his capacity for leadership shows the strength of his character. As the voyage progressed, with its manifold problems not only in running the ship but in taking far-reaching decisions of policy, it became clear that in him a vigorous personality, with an independent and determined mind, had entered the story of African exploration. His modesty prevented him from dramatising his experiences in the style of H. M. Stanley, nor did he ever capture the popular imagination as did Mungo Park or David Livingstone; but in him there was the spirit of the true explorer and of an empire-builder endowed with imagination and humanity.

On joining the ship at Clarence Cove, Fernando Po, the first problem presented itself in the person of Mr Taylor, whom Laird had appointed shipmaster. Baikie was suspicious of the man's capabilities from the start, but a glance at his instructions reassured him. Taylor was there told that the relationship of the Europeans on board the *Pleiad* to him was that "of first-class passengers in a contract steam packet. In case of any difference of opinion, you will require an order in writing from the senior present, and that order you will obey."

Taylor's inefficiency was demonstrated soon after the ship entered the maze of rivers in the delta. The native pilot wished to pass to port of a rock lying in midstream. Taylor was too slow to make up his mind to follow his advice, so that the *Pleiad* ran right on the rock. Such irresolution confirmed Baikie's opinion that "he was not adapted for the work." He was obviously a muddler, a lazy commander who was constantly quarrelling with his subordinates, and an incompetent administrator of the stores on board. Nor did he approve of working on what he called "the Sabbath". It was only after long arguments that the mate was permitted to warp the vessel off by means of a kedge anchor.

A fortnight later much the same thing happened again, when the ship ran aground in shallow water. Taylor explained that it was impossible to go on. Baikie told him that unless he did so he would relieve him of the command of the ship and would, with the mate's assistance, take her up the river himself. Not expecting such a sharp reply, Taylor temporised by suggesting that they should all go below to discuss that matter in his cabin. "As I continued firm in my determination, he made up his mind to get out of his scrape with the best grace he could, announcing that for peace sake he would yield the point, and dropping some hints, meant to be awfully significant, about mutiny and piracy, retired to his beloved couch and cigar."

More delays and disputes followed. After thirty-six days on the river Baikie decided to make an end to this continual squabbling. Feeling himself fully justified in assuming responsibility for the voyage, he ordered the mate to replace Taylor as shipmaster and navigator, while he himself took executive control.

By this time they had reached the confluence of the Benue with the Niger, where, below the green-topped Mount Stirling, the Model Farm had been purchased thirteen years ago. A marvellous wide panorama of the two great rivers uniting in a landscape dotted with flourishing villages opened before them. "Far as the eye could reach, over miles and miles, the ground teemed with exuberant vegetation; seeming often in the fantastic appearance of its wild growth to revel in its exemption from culture. Such a fruitful soil in other climes, and with a happier population, would yield support and employment to countless thousands, and long ere this have proved a source of untold wealth. To complete our panorama, quietly at anchor, and now surrounded by canoes, there lay the little *Pleiad*, the avant-courière of European energy and influence; and I trust the forerunner of civilisation and its attendant blessings, and of better days to these richly-endowed but hitherto unfortunate regions."

Baikie saw at once that the site chosen for the Model Farm

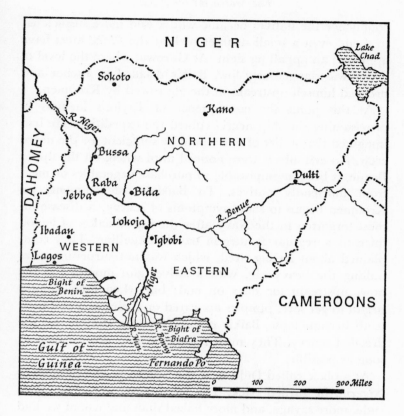

was wrong, because it lay too near the stretch of marshland formed by the junction of the two rivers. On the other side, however, at Igbobi there was a promising site where Bishop Crowther later established his first mission station.

As the *Pleiad* steamed up the Benue, which it was their primary purpose to explore, the scenery increased in beauty. By August 18 they had reached Dagbo, the furthest point reached by the *Alburkha*, but a long way below the point where Barth had crossed the river on his way to Yola. From there onwards the river narrowed, the navigation became treacherous and instead of the friendly villagers of the confluence the natives became wilder and more suspicious; to them, even a small steamer such as the *Pleiad* must have appeared an appalling sight. At Gurowa, where the level of water was dangerously low, Baikie decided to anchor and proceed himself upstream in the gig rowed by Kroomen.

At this point the consequence of Taylor's laziness in provisioning the ship nearly ruined the expedition. He had imagined that a diet of rice would be sufficient for the negro crew. No evil effects were noticed until when, on the upper Benue, it became impossible to purchase vegetables or meat from unfriendly natives. To Baikie's astonishment, his Kroomen began to show symptoms of scurvy, a disease almost forgotten in the Navy after the introduction of lemon juice as a regular feature in naval victualling. They complained about feeling tired, which was not surprising after pulling the heavy gig, with a swivel gun mounted in the bow, upstream for days on end; but when their mouths began to get sore, pimples appeared on their gums and their teeth became loose, Baikie realised that the trouble was the dreaded scurvy. They must rejoin the ship downstream as soon as possible.

At a place called Dulti near the eastern border of modern Nigeria, he turned back. The inhabitants were "far more rude, more savage, and more naked than any whom we had encountered." When trying to land, a fleet of canoes suddenly appeared to attack them, each canoe carrying from eight to ten men. The frightened Kroomen pulled as hard as their weakness allowed in order to escape from the creek into the open river.

"Not knowing how matters might terminate, we thought it advisable to prepare for defence, so I took our revolver to load it, but now, when it was needed, the ramrod was stiff and quite immoveable. Mr May got a little pocket pistol ready, and we had if required a cutlass and a ship's musket, which the Kroomen, by this time in a desperate fright, wished to see prepared, as they kept calling to us 'Load de big gun, load de big gun!' Could an unconcerned spectator have witnessed the scene, he would have been struck by the amount of the ludicrous it contained. There were our Kru boys, as pale as black men could be, the perspiration starting from every pore, exerting to the utmost of their powerful muscles, while Mr May and I were trying to look as unconcerned as possible and, to lessen the indignity of our retreat, were smiling and bowing to the Dulti people, and beckoning them to follow us. Their light canoes were very narrow, and the people were obliged to stand upright. The blades of their paddles, instead of being the usual lozenge shape, were oblong and rectangular and all curved in the direction of the propelling stroke. It was almost a regatta, our gig taking and keeping the lead. Ahead we saw an opening in the bush by which we hoped to make our final retreat, but we were prepared, should the boat take the ground, to jump out and shove her into deep water. Fortune favoured us, we reached the doubtful spot, and with a single stroke of our paddles shot into the open river. Here we knew we were comparatively safe, as if the natives tried to molest us, all we had to do was to give their canoes the stem and so upset them. Our pursuers apparently guessed that we had now got the advantage, as they declined following us into the river, but turning back paddled to their watery abodes, and so ended the grand Dulti chase."

The gig returned to Garowa to find the *Pleiad* gone, presumably in order to avoid the danger of being stranded when the water level fell. After an anxious day's search, she was located twenty miles downstream already aground and it was with much difficulty that the scurvy-ridden crew ever got her off.

On October 20 they reached the confluence again. Baikie had the satisfaction of knowing that he had reached a point several hundred miles higher than that previously attained, and that he could now buy fresh meat and vegetables to restore his crew to health. But in the other object of the expedition – to make contact with Barth – he had failed. Enquiries at all the villages up the Benue merely elicited rumours that two white men had been seen further north. No wonder, because Barth had come south of Lake Chad two years ago, though he was now on his way to Timbuktu.

The return voyage of the *Pleiad* to Fernando Po was uneventful. Beyond enjoying once more the scenery at the confluence and noting the intelligence of its inhabitants, there is no hint in Baikie's narrative of the prospect of his spending the last ten years of his life there. He is far more insistent on the importance of Fernando Po, which was for a time occupied by the British. "Such an island would be considered an acquisition anywhere, but situated as it is, it must be looked on as destined by Providence to play a very important part in the great work of African Regeneration." However, on account of the island's evil reputation for health, it was Lagos which was to be the point of entry for British influence in the Niger area.

Baikie returned to England on February 3, 1855. A synopsis of what was to be his narrative of the expedition was sent directly to the Foreign Office while he himself prepared the book for publication in his spare time at Haslar Hospital. *A Narrative of an Exploring Voyage up the Rivers Kwo'ra and Bi'nue (commonly known as the Niger and Tsadda)* appeared in 1856, that is to say, before the publication of Barth's book. Its conclusion contains proposals for the exploitation of his success, which are echoed in Baikie's correspondence with the government:

"We can confidently point out for those who follow a fresh field for energy and activity, an unbroken ground, where both honour and riches may be reaped. . . . Gifted as we have been with a revelation from on high, it is only our duty to impart its doctrines to our less favoured brethren, and a great – a noble task is in store for those who will pioneer the way of civilization and Christianity. . . . Convince them [the inhabitants] how much happier it would be for all to rest quietly under their own vines and fig-trees, where there would be none to make them afraid, than, as at present being in daily, nay, hourly dread of being carried off into captivity by some more powerful than themselves. Thus a promise of regular trade, of commercial establishments, of an uninterrupted supply of European goods, would form legitimate bribes for good behaviour, and one which would exercise great influence. Let but these tribes once experience even for a short time the comfort of such a new mode of life, and I hardly think that they would again return to their former ways. . . . I am no advocate for endeavouring to acquire new territory; on the contrary, I think such a proceeding would be prejudicial to our views. We should go to Africa as we would to other foreign countries, as visitors, as traders, or as settlers, doing what we could to improve the race by precept and by practice, but avoiding any violent interference or physical demonstration. . . . No auxiliary is more effectual than commerce, which, to minds constituted like those of the Africans, is highly intelligible. The country is promising, the people are favourable, and the way, though not absolutely free from danger, is open and not difficult. Thousands will hail our advent, and in after-ages our first attempt to visit and to improve these regions will occupy a bright page in African history."

The brightest page which Baikie wrote was relegated to an appendix, though it was developed in a long and as yet unpublished treatise now in the British Museum. This was his demonstration of the prophylactic value of quinine by the fact that not one of the twelve Europeans on board the *Pleiad* died of fever. This was an unprecedented record in the history of the exploration of the Niger.

Contemporary medical knowledge was incapable of solving the problem of causation. After deploring current attempts to sub-divide fevers as merely calculated to puzzle and mislead, Baikie proceeds: "While up the Niger in 1854 I had ample opportunity of testing this virtue [of quinine], and I most unhesitatingly record my belief in its existence. . . . I can affirm that after taking my morning dose (2–4 gr.) I felt fit for any kind of duty, all the languour of a close damp tropical night was dispelled, or in the evening after a hard day's work in the hot sun, nothing was so reviving and exhilarating as this invaluable drug." In his printed account he claimed that "the great modern improvement is the discovery that quinine not only cures, but that it actually prevents, and that by taking this invaluable drug while in unhealthy localities, persons may escape totally unscathed. The best form for use for this purpose is quinine wine, of which half a glass should be taken early in the morning and repeated if requisite in the afternoon. Drugs should be avoided as much as possible, especially calomel and other mercurials, which are not only unnecessary, but have actually killed far more people than fever ever has. . . . We find Malaria nearly ubiquitous, though more prevalent in warm climates. But in no *essential* does African endemic fever differ from the fever of Hindustan, of Borneo, of the Spanish Main, of the West Indies, or of fenny or marshy countries in Europe. The treatment required is the same; only as the symptoms are more violent, so should the remedies be more decided and more quickly pushed."

While he was writing his book he was also bombarding the Foreign Office with plans for another expedition. So were Laird and Crowther, the last of whom expressed his belief that "the time is fully come when Christianity must be introduced on the banks of the Niger." Baikie's own views were based on the argument that trade was what the African understood and appreciated. The resettlement of slaves who came from that part of Africa might help, but commerce was the most likely means of communication.

As a result of these appeals, another Admiralty contract for an annual vessel was signed with Laird in 1857. On May 2 the *Dayspring*, of only 77 tons, powered by a 30 h.p. engine, sailed from Liverpool with Baikie on board. There were also Crowther, Dalton (the zoologist of the first expedition who became Baikie's friend for life) and a crew of eleven men; and there was Lieutenant J. H. Glover of the Hydrographical Department of the Admiralty. Aged thirty-one, he was fired with the same ideals as the others. On his first view of the confluence he wrote:

"The river winding its way brought some sad thoughts to my mind. From all its various sources till its entrance into the sea, Oppression, Bloodshed, Wrong and Darkness blot with foul spots its splendid stream. A fatality seems to hang over it. May it please God that we shall aid in its removal and soon Commerce as the means to a greater end may cover its waters with other burdens than slaves and the results of war and depredation."

The *Dayspring* reached the confluence on August 10, only thirty-three days from the sea. After spending a short time at Igbobi, where Crowther established his mission, Baikie pushed on upstream until on October 7 the little vessel was swept by the current on to what was called the ju-ju rock near Jebba. For exactly a year twelve Europeans and thirty-eight Krumen were stranded at Rabba on the eastern bank. At least, Baikie told the Foreign Office afterwards, "one result of our long stay ashore is to show that with ordinary care Europeans may live with impunity in Central Africa under very disadvantageous conditions."

It was Glover who made the most of those months. Seven hundred miles of the lower Niger were surveyed, and when he went upstream in a canoe to Bussa he had the good fortune to find in the possession of the chief a tattered

nautical almanack which was stolen from Mungo Park and
is now his sole surviving relic in England. Glover also noticed
that the chief wore on his finger a medal which was obviously
another relic, but this he could not obtain. Until recently it
was still worn by the chief of Bussa. Glover was thus the first
white man to travel so far up the river. When he returned to
the disgruntled party at Rabba, he volunteered to go across
country to Lagos and thence by sea to Sierra Leone to fetch
help. After the annexation of Lagos in 1861, he became its
first Governor as Sir John Glover.

At the end of October, 1858 the relief ship *Sunbeam* at last
appeared to take Baikie and his party off. By that time they
were not a happy party. The shipmaster, like Taylor on the
first expedition, bullied the natives. The doctor abetted him
and the mate was later sent home for insubordination:
Laird's choice of officers was no happier than on other
occasions. Only Baikie's quiet authority enabled them to
survive and after their return to Fernando Po he decided to
go back to settle at a place near the confluence which he
called at first Lairdstown, but later adopted the native name
of Lokoja, which (it is said) means "the fine place which
attracts men to it." He had hoped to establish himself as a
consul at Rabba, a much bigger town and the centre of the
market on the route north to Sokoto, but he found that the
slave traders of the delta had warned the Emir against him.
The latter, however, presented him with the site at Lokoja,
where, with occasional journeys overland to Lagos in one
direction and Kano in another, he remained for the rest of
his life.

It was only gradually that he learned to accept his isolation
up river. A sad letter to Murchison, now President of the
Royal Geographical Society, (by whose permission it is now
printed) which is dated October 18, 1859, explains why he
cannot contribute anything to the Society's journal.

"I work now daily, without intermission except when

prevented by actual sickness, from 14 to 16 hours a day, and the effects in this climate can hardly be described. I am at work by early daylight, and seldom give over till near midnight, when I am entirely exhausted. I have not been in anything like a bed for more than two years. I have had fever on more than 120 separate occasions, not reckoning mere recurrences after intermission, but so many distinct attacks. . . . Secondly, I have found that what I have written home excites but little interest. I have collected information of all sorts, have offered plans and made suggestions, but they are not noticed. I receive no support, no approbation, not even disapprobation. This, sir, I think you will admit is not very encouraging. I have incurred the hostility of the slave traders on the coast, and I have been told that I am in bad odour among what may be called Exeter Hall people, because I would not lend myself to some ultra-missionary ideas. I have had much opposition among my own people because my view of duty was looked upon as too strict. I cannot venture for a moment to compete with a Livingstone or a Barth, and my duties are much more political than theirs and therefore less interesting, but I hope if I am spared to reach home I shall be able to show that my time has not been idly spent."

The chief drawback to life at Lokoja was not isolation but the hostility of the delta peoples, a very different type to Baikie's and Barth's Muslim friends in the north; and also of the Liverpool traders on the coast. The outpost was often cut off for months at a time when Laird's steamers were attacked by these ferocious savages, about whom Baikie wrote in strong terms to his government:

"Mr Laird was perfectly correct when he defined 'moral force in Africa' as meaning a 32-pounder with an English sailor standing behind it. Expostulations or threats are alike misunderstood or uncared for by such complete savages, and nothing less than the summary destruction of several of their towns will have any effect upon them. It cannot be that such a worthless set of mere brutes, so few, too, in numbers, should continue practically to close the mouth of a large river, flowing along half of a vast continent. . . . Until the river shall be re-opened by a couple of heavy guns energetically worked, I have no road for communications or supplies but the very long circuitous one from this place to Lagos."

The Foreign Office agreed, but the Admiralty did not. In their view "Trade enforced by cannon shot will take no root." To which the Foreign Office replied, "Our experience proves the contrary." The Commodore of the Bight's squadron refused to co-operate, because he claimed to have an insufficient squadron to continue the anti-slavery patrols as well as sending a gunboat through such a notoriously hostile area. To which Lord John Russell replied (as Baikie had long argued) that "It would be worth while to consider whether it would not be desirable to take possession of Lagos without delay. Such a measure could not fail to have great effect on the minds of the natives of the Delta." Gunboat diplomacy of this sort would certainly placate the abolitionist lobby in London. After Lagos was indeed formally annexed, the consequences were exactly as predicted.

Meanwhile Baikie's settlement was thriving, chiefly because he had won the confidence of Masaba, Emir of Nupe and all the country north of the confluence. As he told a friend, "Masaba has placed the general charge of the district in my hands to keep peace, and I have already settled several disputes which threatened to lead to war and bloodshed. Natives are beginning to gather round me, as they consider themselves safe under our protection and with a little encouragement this will become a great and busy town." Nevertheless, he and Dalton, the zoologist, remained isolated at Lokoja either when the level of the river was too low for the steamers, or when they were attacked in the delta. Not until the end of August, 1861 did the *Sunbeam* arrive again, by which time Baikie had spent all his money, sold his clothes and existed by the charity of Masaba on three-pence a day. "I would submit to any privations rather than give up what has cost us so much labour and what promises so well."

When the next ship reached him it carried a notice of recall, penned at Whitehall a year previously. He was in no mood to submit. "I venture to defer my return," he politely informed the Foreign Secretary, until the government was better informed of the situation. It did not appear that the flourishing state of his settlement was appreciated in White-hall, nor the importance of the job he was doing: "What I look to are the securing for England of a commanding position in Central Africa, and the necessity for making a commencement." Dalton was sent home because his health was poor and the ship was ordered to return as soon as she had landed supplies, but Baikie himself stayed on for another three years. It is no wonder that he turned native. He was an excellent linguist, translating the Book of Genesis (of all things) into Hausa, compiling a grammar of the Fulde language, and writing endless despatches (which have not hitherto been printed) to an uninterested Foreign Office. He was now running one of the most successful markets on the Niger. He was trusted by the Emir. He had fallen in love with native life to the extent of almost forgetting to speak his own language or wear his own clothes.

A trader who met him at this time says that he wore the turban, the long cotton shirt called a *tobe*, the baggy trousers and sandals of a Muslim. He had a black mistress and fathered several children, so that it is said that even today little boys hail the appearance of a European in those parts with cries of Bekki, Bekki!

Not until 1864 did he agree to return by one of the river steamers. He was accompanied by several Africans, three of whom – Aaron, Joseph and Harry – bore his name. As he had been in the habit of purchasing slave boys at 12/6 a head, these can hardly have been his sons, and after he died of dysentery at Sierra Leone on the voyage home, they were sent back to their native Niger.

Baikie's papers were entrusted by the Foreign Office to John Kirk, the friend of Livingstone, who had done so much to establish British influence on the east coast. After perusing Baikie's diary, Kirk wrote:

"Poor Baikie was in a strange state of mind – no doubt being complicated with native women and a young family of half-castes induced there. That he was on the right course there can be no doubt and to me the wonder is that no nation has taken up the regular trade in those regions. As a colony it will never do, nor will any tropical African station, but Lokoja was probably more healthy than the settlements we hold and would be more influential. Those who know what it is to be alone in savage parts will readily understand why Baikie's health failed, cut off as he was from the outer world and without the excitement of discovery and travel which we had during six years on the opposite coast."

In another letter, regretting Baikie's failure to return after his "long banishment", Kirk said that he had plotted the route of the journey to Kano for the benefit of the Royal Geographical Society, because this was through an untravelled area. Baikie's notes, as edited by Kirk, therefore appeared in the Society's journal in 1867. More important, perhaps, was the opportunity Baikie had provided at Lokoja for British traders. As for the doctor himself, Kirk concluded, "it is not to be supposed that a single European will again be shut out from all assistance for so long a time as he was, or exposed to the same hardships. . . . In him Africa has lost a true, devoted and eminently practical friend, and the nation a zealous, self-denying servant." Curiously enough, he rejected what is surely Baikie's chief title to fame, his proof of the efficacy of quinine. Whatever its benefits as a cure, thought Kirk, it seemed valueless as a preventive. But as a modern historian of British policy in North and West Africa, Dr Boahen, has suggested, his demonstration of "the prophylactic use of quinine made the Niger rather than the Sahara the obvious route to the Sudan. The failure of attempts to develop British commerce, the fear of alienating the French, and the ineffectiveness of the Murzuk vice-consulate in the crusade against the Saharan slave trade – all these factors brought about the withdrawal of the British from the Sahara and the region of Timbuktu, and the concentration of their efforts on the Niger–Benue axis. This withdrawal paved the way for the birth of what became to be known as the French Sahara and French West and Equatorial Africa on the one hand, and of British Nigeria on the other."

The Emir Masaba was informed in a personal letter from Queen Victoria of his friend Baikie's death. The Queen promised to replace him with another consul, but the latter was withdrawn three years later and in the anti-imperialist mood of mid-Victorian England even Crowther was brought down from his mission station.

The Queen stressed the fact that England was only interested in suppressing the traffic in slaves. "We ask your Highness to use your great influence to put a stop to this traffic, and to prevent the wars that are undertaken in many cases for the sole purpose of procuring slaves to be sold for shipment overseas. . . . We request you to accept our best wishes and so we recommend you to the protection of the Almighty. Given at our Court at Osborne the 20th July, 1865, in the 29th year of our reign. Your good friend, VICTORIA."

That same year the government accepted the notorious recommendation of a Select Committee that Britain should withdraw from West Africa. This recommendation has been seriously misunderstood, as far as the Niger area is concerned.

The men who made it were Free Traders opposed to what they regarded as the waste of money involved in the maintenance of forts and trading establishments of the type favoured by Laird and Baikie. They were more interested in the Gold Coast than in the Niger, where, as Dr Dike has shown, not only did no withdrawal take place but trade developed steadily, if slowly. The consulate at Lokoja might be closed down, but traders on the coast flourished all the more. What happened was really no more than a change of emphasis: instead of encouraging trade in the interior, the government left those coastal traders, who had always opposed "a Niger subsidy", a free hand.

In Baikie's day, as we have seen, the Foreign Office demanded and received Admiralty assistance in protecting trade up river. As Russell said, the government was determined "to establish and develop permanent commercial intercourse by this route with the interior of Africa," and Baikie was directed to inform the river chiefs that their countries would be visited regularly. The consequence was that no less than five trading companies were founded in the next few years, the success of which aroused the jealousy of the coastal traders, who wished to preserve a monopoly of the palm oil exports. The latter faction triumphed in 1865, when the Select Committee made its recommendation, but the logic of Baikie's achievement meant an increase in trade generally. Commerce in the river, backed by sea power, was bound to promote the cause of trade on the Niger, especially as the rulers on its banks could no longer depend, as they had done for so long, on the slave trade alone.

The man who swung the pendulum back to Lokoja and the interior of Africa was George (later Sir George) Dashwood Taubman Goldie, who arrived in the delta in 1877. There he found intense and wasteful competition between the freebooters. Within two years he had knocked their heads together to form the United African Company, which became in turn the National African Company, the Royal Niger Company and eventually Nigeria.

The age of the explorers ended with Baikie's death. That of the traders, financiers, soldiers and statesmen began with Goldie, the empire builder. The French were advancing down the upper Niger, and from Algeria into the Sahara. The Germans, in a surprise move, annexed the Cameroons. But thanks to Baikie's foundations at what he originally called Lairdstown in honour of the chief pioneer of trade on the river, Goldie was now firmly entrenched at Lokoja. On his first journey back from that place he wrote, "I conceived the ambition of adding the region of the Niger to the British Empire." He made the place what Baikie intended – "the commanding position in Central Africa", so that at the Congress of Berlin in 1885 the lower Niger was accepted as a British sphere of influence.

Thereafter the territories bordering the river which have been described in this book were arbitrarily divided into French and British and German colonies during the sordid horse-dealing sometimes called the Scramble for Africa. A line running east from Timbuktu and Say to Lake Chad divided the French zone from the British, one from the upper Benue down to the coast the British from the German. Such lines drawn on a map in Europe bore no relation to the agglomeration of tribes, peoples and religions which so perplexed the pioneers we have been considering. What the Franco-British line meant in practice was that most of the empire of Sokoto fell within the British sphere, so that Goldie's successor, the real architect of modern Nigeria – Lord Lugard – had to defeat the Sultan's troops in battle. What would Dr Barth have said about the storming of the walls of Kano by negro troops under British officers?

Just as Goldie chose Lokoja as the base for his trading company, Lugard used it for his military forces when he came to establish British rule in the territories of the Royal

Niger Company. It was there that his West African Frontier Force was raised in 1898. Today Lokoja continues to be what the pioneers had hoped – a flourishing centre of trade, a busy river port, and the site of vast oil storage tanks where mineral oil has replaced palm oil as the principal source of wealth on the Niger.

Chronology of Principal Events

1788	Foundation of African Association
1788	Death of Ledyard at Cairo
1789	Death of Hornemann near Niger
1790	Death of Houghton from Gambia
1795	Mungo Park's first expedition to Segu
1805	Park's second expedition and death at Bussa
1816	Tuckey's expedition to the Congo
1818	Ritchie and Lyon to Fezzan
1819–21	Gray's expedition from Gambia
1822–25	Denham, Clapperton and Oudney to Lake Chad and Sokoto
1824–26	Gordon Laing to Timbuktu
1825–28	René Caillié to Timbuktu and Fez
1825	Clapperton's second expedition with Lander to Sokoto and death
1831	Amalgamation of African Association with Geographical Society
1830–32	The Landers travel down the Niger from Bussa to its mouth
1832–34	Voyage of Laird, Oldfield, Lander and Allen to Rabba; death of Lander
1841	Voyage up Niger by Allen and Thompson
1849–55	Travels of Barth from Tripoli, Chad to Timbuktu and back
1854	Baikie's first expedition up Benue
1857–64	Baikie's residence at Lokoja
1864	Death of Baikie

Sources

I. THE MYSTERY OF THE NIGER

Robin Hallett, *The Penetration of Africa to 1805* (*1965*)
Robin Hallett (ed.), *The Records of the African Association* (*1964*)
E. W. Bovill, *The Niger Explored* (*1968*)
A. A. Boahen, *Britain, the Sahara and the Western Soudan* (*1964*)
C. Howard and J. H. Plumb (ed.), *West African Explorers* (*1951*)
C. Lloyd and J. L. S. Coulter, *Medicine and the Navy*, vols. iii, iv
   (*1961*)

2. MUNGO PARK'S FIRST EXPEDITION

Mungo Park, *Travels in the Interior Districts of Africa* (*1799*, and
   Everyman Library)
Hallett, op. cit.
Boahen, op. cit.

3. THE DEATH OF MUNGO PARK

Mungo Park, op. cit. Everyman edition
Hallett, op. cit.
Public Record Office C.O. 2/1

4. THE ATTACK FROM THE NORTH

E. W. Bovill, *Missions to the Niger*, Hakluyt Society, 4 vols. (*1964*)
E. Denham, H. Clapperton and W. Oudney, *Narrative of Travels
   and Discoveries in Northern and Central Africa* (*1828*)
René Caillié, *Travels through Central Africa to Timbuctoo* (*1830*)
G. F. Lyon, *Narrative of Travels in Northern Africa* (*1821*)
J. K. Tuckey, *Narrative of an Expedition to Explore the River Zaire*
   (*1818*)

Sources

W. Gray, *Travels in Western Africa in the years 1818–1821* (*1825*)
Quarterly Review, 1821
Bonnel de Mezières, *Le Major Gordon Laing* (Paris, *1912*)
C. Lloyd, *Mr Barrow of the Admiralty* (*1970*)
Hallett, op. cit.
Boahen, op. cit.

5. HUGH CLAPPERTON

Public Record Office C.O. 2/13, 14, 16, 17 and 324/76
Bovill, *Missions to the Niger*, op. cit.
H. Clapperton, *Journal of a Second Expedition into the Interior of Africa* (*1829*)
R. Lander, *Records of Captain Clapperton's Last Expedition in Africa* (*1830*)
Quarterly Review, 1826

6. THE MYSTERY SOLVED (THE LANDERS)

R. and J. Lander, *Journal of an Expedition to Explore the Course and Termination of the Niger* (*1830*); there is a good modern edition of selections edited by R. Hallett
Public Record Office C.O. 2/16, 18
K. O. Dike, *Trade and Politics in the Niger Delta* (*1956*)
Lloyd and Coulter, *Medicine and the Navy*, vol. iv., op. cit.
Quarterly Review, 1832

7. UPSTREAM (LAIRD AND OLDFIELD)

Macgregor Laird and R. A. Oldfield, *Narrative of an Expedition into the Interior of Africa by the River Niger* (*1837*)
W. Allen, *Picturesque Views of the River Niger* (*1840*)
J. McQueen, *A Geographical and Commercial View of Northern Central Africa* (*1822*)
P. D. Curtin, "The White Man's Grave: Image and Reality" in *Journal of British Studies, 1961*
H. H. Scott, *History of Tropical Medicine* (*1939*)
Lloyd and Coulter, op. cit., vol. iv
C. C. Lloyd, *The Navy and the Slave Trade* (*1949*)

R. Robinson, J. Gallacher, A. Denny, *Africa and the Victorians*
(*1961*)
Dike, op. cit.
Geographical Journal, 1861

8. THE SECOND ATTEMPT (ALLEN AND TROTTER)

T. Fowell Buxton, *The African Slave Trade and its Remedy* (*1840*)
H. D. Trotter, W. Allen and T. R. H. Thompson, *Narrative of the
Expedition to the River Niger in 1841* (*1848*)
Journals of J. F. Schön and S. Crowther (1842)
J. O. MacWilliam, *Medical History of the Expedition to the Niger*
(*1843*)
R. M. Jackson, *Journal of a Voyage to Bonny River* (*1934*)
W. Gallacher, "Fowell Buxton and the New African Policy" in
Cambridge Historical Journal, vol. X
C. C. Lloyd, *The Navy and the Slave Trade* (*1949*)
Lloyd and Coulter, op. cit., vol. IV
Geographical Journal, 1837, 1861
Public Record Office C.O. 2/21–24. Adm. 7/615. 101/127

9. THE TRAVELS OF DR BARTH

H. Barth, *Travels and Discoveries in North and Central Africa, 5 vols.*,
(*1857–58*)
Ed. A. H. M. Kirk-Greene, *Barth's Travels in Nigeria* (*1962*), with
valuable biographical introduction; see also his contribution
to *Africa and its Explorers*, ed. Robert I. Rotberg (Harvard,
1970)
R. Mansell Prothero, "H. Barth and the Western Soudan" in
Geographical Journal, 1958
E. W. Bovill, "H. Barth" in *Journal of African Society, 1926*
A. Petermann, *An Account of the Progress of the Expedition to Central
Africa*, (*1854*), with portraits
A. Petermann, *A Letter to the President of the Royal Geographical
Society* (*1854*)
J. Richardson, *Narrative of a Mission to Central Africa* (*1853*)
O. A. Boahen, *Britain, the Sahara and the Western Soudan* (*1964*)
H. Schiffer, *H. Barth: Ein Forscher in Afrika* (Wiesbaden, *1967*),
with tribute by Lord Rennell of Rodd

Sources

British Museum, Add. Mss. 32,117E – Barth-Cooley correspondence
Public Record Office. F.O. 101/23–36

10. DR BAIKIE'S SETTLEMENT

W. B. Baikie, *Narrative of an Exploring Voyage up the Rivers Kwora and Binue in 1854 (1856)*
A. C. G. Hastings, *Voyage of the Dayspring (1926)*
S. Crowther, *Journal of an Expedition up the Niger and Tshadda (1855)*
A. Bryson, *Report on the Climate and Principal Diseases of the African Station (1847)*
H. J. Pedroza, *Borrioboola-Gha* (Abadan, *1960*)
O. A. Boahen, op. cit.
Lloyd and Coulter, op. cit., vol. iv
C. Lloyd, *The Navy and the Slave Trade (1949)*
British Museum. Add. Mss. 39,449 (Baikie's treatise)
Public Record Office. F.O. 2/18, 23, 31, 32, 34. 97/433, 435

Index

Abegga, 166
African Association, 26ff; 61
African Company, 14
African Steamship Company, *see*
 Laird
Agades, 169
Albert, 153, 157
Alburkha, 130ff.
Algiers, 66
Allen, Bird, 150
Allen, W., 131, 149ff.
Amadi Fatuma, 55–7
Anderson, A., 50
Anti-slave trade patrols, 95, 142,
 146, 160, 187

Badagry, 95, 109, 111, 189
Baikie, W. B., 116, 190. First
 expedition 190–6; second 198–
 200; and quinine 197; at
 Lokoja 201–3; death 204
Bakay, El, 177–80
Bamako, 52
Banks, Sir J., 26ff.; 46ff.; 62
Barros, J. de, 13
Barrow, Sir J., 16, 61–7, 79, 91,
 94
Barth, H., 59, 161ff.
Bathurst, Lord, 67, 98
Beaufoy, H., 27, 29

Beecroft, J., 138, 152ff.; 188
Bello, Sultan, 88–90, 98, 103
Bencoolen, 31
Benin, 152
Benue, 116, 135, 173, 176, 190,
 192
Boahen, A. A., 205
Bornu, 83, 171
Boy, King, 120–3, 132
Brazen HMS, 92
Bruce, J., 47
Bryson, A., 187
Bussa, 57, 90, 96, 113, 199
Buxton, Sir T. Fowell, 148, 158

Caillié, R., 69ff., 179
Calabar, 137
Camden, Lord, 49
Cape Coast Castle, 111, 132
Catalan map, 18
Chad, Lake, 83, 163, 207
Chesterfield, Lord, 17
Clapperton, H., 58, 68. First
 expedition 77ff.; second ex-
 pedition 91ff.
Clarence Cove, *see* Fernando Po
Columbine, 130
Congo, 50, 63
Congo HMS, 64
Cooley, D., 174

217

Crowther, S., 153, 193, 199, 205

Dalton, J., 199, 202, 203
Damergou, 169
D'Anville, F., 21
Dayspring, 199
De L'Isle, 17
Denham, Dixon, 78ff., 92, 109, 163
Diana, 131
Dickens, C., 187
Dickson, J., 31
Dike, K. O., 206
Dorothea HMS, 64
Dulti, 194
Durogu, 167, 185

Eboe (Aboh), 139, 154
Edrisi, El, 16, 19
Edwards, J. B., 27, 46
Encyclopaedia Britannica, 13
Esk HMS, 109
Ethiope, 152, 158

Fernando Po, 22, 123, 138, 143, 196
Fever, pathology of, 22, 126, 151, 188; *see* Quinine
Fez, 76
Fulani, 35
Fundah, 90, 95, 105, 136
Futa Jallon, 28, 33

Gambia, 15, 30, 33, 65
Geographical Society (Royal), 28, 58, 124, 184
Ghadames, 68, 180
Ghana, 18

Glover, Sir J., 58, 189, 199
Gogo (Geo), 180
Goldie, Sir G., 206, 207
Goree, 48, 50
Gray, W., 65

Hillman, W., 79, 87
Hobart, Lord, 48
Hornemann, F., 60
Houghton, 30, 38

Igbobi, 193, 199
Isaaco, 51ff.

Jackson, R. M., 152
Jamieson, R., 152
Jarra, 38
Jenne, 40, 72
Jobson, R., 34
Joliba HMS, 55

Kanemi, El, 83
Kano, 87, 97, 98, 104, 169, 170, 200, 207
Katunga, *see* Oyo
Kirk, Sir J., 204
Kroomen, 132, 134, 153, 194
Kuka (Kukawa), 83, 91, 171, 174

Lagos, 189, 200
Laidley, Dr, 32, 44
Laing, Gordon, 57, 66ff., 74, 177
Lake, Capt., 121
Laird, Macgregor, 125ff., 148, 189, 190, 201
Lander, R. and J. With Clapper-

ton, 93ff.; return journey 103ff.; second expedition 110ff.; third expedition 131ff.; death 140
Leake, H. J., 154
Ledyard, J., 29
Leo Africanus, 16, 20
Lind, J., 23
Livingstone, D., 161
Lokoja, 116, 156, 201, 204, 207
Lucas, S., 29
Lugard, Lord, 207
Lyon, G. F., 61

Maclean, Governor, 132
McQueen, J., 128
MacWilliam, J. O., 150, 157
Mali, 18
Mandingos, 35
Mansong, King, 37, 40, 53
Masaba, Emir, 202, 205
Matra, J., 26, 29
Matson, H. J., 111
Mead, R., 22
Mercator, G., 17
Moore, F., 15
Murchison, Sir R., 185, 190, 200
Murray, J., 125
Murzuk, 60, 81, 163, 166, 205

New South Wales, 48
Nicolls, E., 137, 138
Niger, course and names of, 16, 20, 21, 50, 75, 94, 171
Nupe (Nyffe), 97, 114, 202

Obi of Ibo, 119, 134, 154, 158
Oldfield, R. A. K., 132ff., 152
Oudney, W., 78ff.

Overweg, A., 164, 174
Owen, F. W. F., 24, 123
Oyo (Katunga), 96, 106, 113

Palm oil, 129, 142, 208
Palmerston, Lord, 160, 162, 164
Park, Mungo, 15, 16, 68, 200. First expedition 27ff.; second expedition 46ff.
Parry, Sir E., 150
Pasko *or* Pascoe, 93, 111, 132
Peddie, J., 65
Petermann, A., 184, 186
Pisania, 32, 44, 51
Pleiad, 190
Pory, J., 11, 20
Pritchett, W. M., 151

Quakers, 25, 28, 148
Quinine, 23, 111, 127, 151, 188, 197
Quorra, 130ff.

Rabba, 60, 114, 135, 139, 152, 199
Reichard, Dr, 63
Reid, Dr, 150
Rennell, J., 25, 28, 46, 50
Rennell, Lord, 161
Richardson, J., 162ff.
Ritchie, Major, 61
Ritter, C., 163
Royal Niger Company, 206
Russell, Lord John, 149, 160, 202

Sansanding, 54
Say, 176

Schön, Rev. J. F., 153, 155, 157, 185
Scott, Sir W., 47
Segu, 39
Senegal, 15
Shari, 85, 173
Sierra Leone, 22
Slave Trade, 18, 127, 147. Abolition of, 25, 129, 163, 185. *See* Anti-slave trade patrols
Smythe, W. H., 65
Sokoto, 87, 101, 176, 207
Soudan, 153, 157
Stanger, Dr, 157, 158
Stephen, J., 149
Stevenson, Col, 48
Stirling, Mt, 135, 156, 192
Sturge, J., 147
Sunbeam, 200
Susan, 132
Swift, J., 21

Timbuktu, 20, 69, 73, 76, 177–80, 207
Tripoli, 61, 65, 67, 79, 165, 182
Trotter, H. Dundas, 150ff.
Tshadda, *see* Benue

Tuareg, 35, 74, 179
Tuckey, J. K., 63
Tyrwhitt, J., 79, 86

Vogel, Dr, 181

Wangara, 18, 21
Warrington, Frederick, 164, 167
Warrington, Hanmer, 66ff., 77, 91, 105
Webb, W. H., 158
Wilberforce, W., 25
Wilberforce, 153, 157, 158
Wilson, J., 23
Winterbottom, T., 23
Wowow, 96, 106

Yauri, 56, 58, 114, 181
Yeou (Yobe), 83, 85
Yola, 173
Yoruba, 105

Zair, *see* Congo
Zuma, widow, 96, 106, 113